Table of Contents

The Art of Controlling Love

A memoir by Umair

Introduction

Love is an unstoppable force – it molds, tests and redefines us. But as potent as love is, it demands certain control. This book chronicles my journey through love's highs and lows, revealing the strength found in harnessing its power.

"The Art of Controlling Love" explores the delicate balance between passion and restraint. Each chapter reveals how different forms of love influenced my life and how I learned to guide it, ensuring it fueled my journey without leading me astray.

THIS IS THE ART OF understanding love; shaping it before it shapes you.

The Prologue

The sun had barely begun its descent, casting a golden hue over the sprawling cityscape of London. From where I sat, the city pulsed with life—cars honking in the distance, people hurrying below, unaware of the quiet figure perched atop one of the tallest buildings in the city. The air was crisp, with a slight breeze that tugged gently at the loose strands of my graying hair.

I took a slow sip from a steaming cup of coffee in my hand, the warmth contrasting with the cool evening air. Beside me, a gun rested against the rough concrete of the rooftop ledge. Its presence was as familiar as it was heavy, a silent witness to the years that had brought me to this moment. The weight of it reminded me of the many battles—both literal and metaphorical—I had fought over the decades.

London had always been a city of contradictions—beauty and chaos, history and modernity, peace and conflict. As I looked out over the skyline, I couldn't help but feel that my life had mirrored this city in so many ways. A life filled with triumphs and failures, joys and sorrows, love and learnings.

The book signing waits in the event hall. The irony wasn't lost on me—a life lay bare in ink, now bound between two covers for all to see. I had spent the better part of a year writing that book, distilling six decades of life into a few hundred pages. And now, as the time approached to share it with the world, I found myself on this rooftop, alone with my thoughts.

My reverie was interrupted by the sound of footsteps approaching. I turned to see Edward making his way towards me. At twenty-five, Edward has a strong presence with a commanding stature and an earnest expression that reflects both his youth and the weight of his responsibilities. His dark hair, neatly trimmed, and his sharp features give him a distinguished look, while his eyes, a deep and thoughtful brown, convey a mix of concern and determination.

"Dad," he said. His voice carrying a note of urgency, "it's time for the book signing. Everyone is waiting for you."

Before I could respond, Elsa and Sophia joined us on the terrace. Elsa, with her striking auburn hair and a hint of mischief in her eyes, wore a vibrant red dress. Sophia, calm and composed as always, was dressed in a simple blue top and jeans. Their presence brought a sense of warmth to the cool evening.

Elsa's eyes were drawn to the gun with a mix of apprehension and intrigue, while Sophia stood a step behind her sister, her gaze shifting between the gun and me.

"It's a beautiful evening," I said softly, breaking the silence. My voice was steady, but there was a hint of nostalgia as I spoke.

They nodded, their eyes never straying far from me or the gun.

Edward, with his sharp features and thoughtful demeanor, is a young man who exudes a quiet strength that mirrors his inner resilience. His dark, wavy hair falls naturally, framing a face that carries a blend of both his mother's gentle grace and my own more rugged countenance. His eyes, deep and expressive, often reflect an inner world rich with contemplation and empathy, qualities that have always set him apart. There's a certain maturity in his gaze, a wisdom that seems beyond his years, yet there's also softness—an enduring kindness that hints at the deep well of emotions he carefully guards.

Standing beside him, it's impossible not to feel a sense of pride and warmth. Our bond has always been one of unspoken understanding, a connection forged through the trials we've faced together. From the early days when he would clumsily grip my hand as we walked, to the present, where a simple exchange of glances is enough to convey volumes, our relationship has grown into something profound. Edward has inherited not just my features but also my temperament—steady, thoughtful, and always a bit reflective. There's an unbreakable thread between us, woven from shared experiences, mutual respect, and a deep, unwavering love. It's a bond that has weathered storms, one that continues to strengthen as we navigate the complexities of life side by side.

Elsa, with her striking resemblance to her mother, carried an aura of elegance mixed with a lively, playful spirit that was entirely her own. Her eyes, large and expressive, were a captivating shade of deep brown, often sparkling with mischief. She had a smile that could light up a room, and her laughter was infectious, bringing warmth and joy wherever she went.

Her long, wavy hair framed her face perfectly, often tumbling over her shoulders in a carefree manner that reflected her lighthearted personality. Elsa was the type who could turn any serious moment into something fun, her playful taunts and quick wit adding a lightness to even the most intense conversations. She had a knack for knowing just when to tease, just when to joke, making her a delightful presence in our lives.

Her playful nature was more than just charm; it was a reminder that life didn't always have to be so heavy, that even in the midst of life's complexities, there was always room for a bit of laughter and light.

Sophia carries a serene and thoughtful demeanor. Her calm presence is often a grounding force, offering a sense of tranquility that contrasts with the more dynamic aspects of my life. Her innocence and genuine curiosity about the world around her reflect a pure, thoughtful approach to life. Sophia's ability to stay composed and her reflective nature make her a comforting presence, underscoring the deep bond we share. She approaches situations with a quiet strength and a sense of empathy that often brings out a sense of peace and introspection in me.

Sophia's appearance complements her calm and innocent nature. She has soft, curly hair that frames her face, which is round and expressive, radiating a sense of purity and warmth. Her innocent round face often lights up with a gentle smile, reflecting her thoughtful and serene disposition. Her look, combined with her tranquil demeanor, adds to her endearing quality, making her presence both comforting and charming.

Their presence on the terrace marked a perfect time to introduce them with my understanding of love and my journey through the most difficult yet important times of life. The stage of life they are going through is most suited for me to make them understand my words and grasp the lessons, that I learnt the hard way, easily.

"I suppose you're wondering why I'm up here," I continued, my voice gaining warmth as I spoke to them. "And why I have this." I glanced down at the gun, then back at their faces.

Elsa, ever curious, finally spoke up. "Dad, what's going on? Why are you up here with... that?"

"This," I said, tapping the gun lightly, "is a reminder. Of the choices I've made, the paths I've taken, and the person I've become. And this," I lifted the cup of coffee, "is a reminder that despite everything, I'm still here, embracing life"

I paused, looking out at the city again. "There's so much I want to tell you. About my life, about the journey that brought me to this moment. But I don't want you to just hear it—I want you to understand it."

Edward, Elsa, and Sophia exchanged glances. Edward, showcasing his concern about the book signing, spoke up "Dad, Can this wait? We have an event to attend." Me, being me, replied, "This, my son, is the perfect time." They all settled down leaning in slightly as if bracing themselves for the weight of what was to come.

I took a deep breath, the memories flooding back as I prepared to tell them the story of my life—the story of how a young man from modest beginnings became the person sitting before them, with a lifetime of stories, lessons, and triumphs etched into every line on his face.

And so, I began to speak, my words carrying us back to the beginning, to the moments that had shaped not just my life, but the lives of those I loved.

"Let me tell you how it all began..."

Chapter 1: Alice

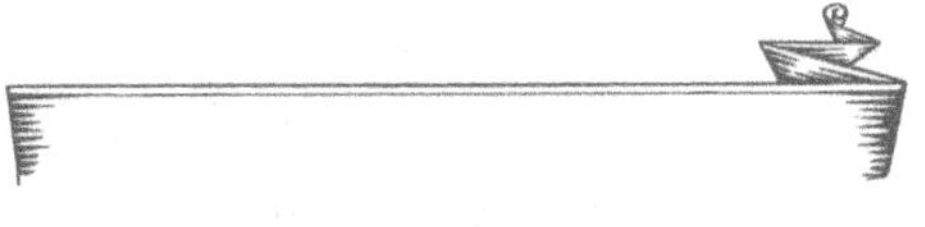

The Realization

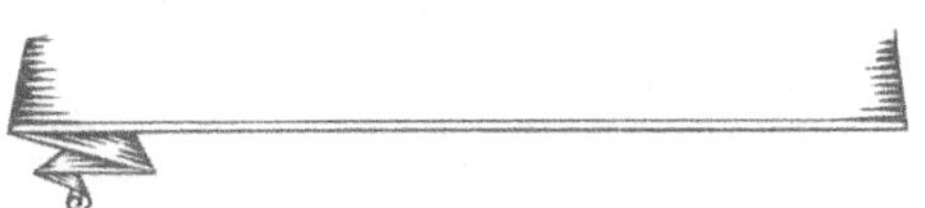

As my youth unfolded, life seemed to glide along effortlessly, bathed in the golden hues of endless possibilities. The days were marked by carefree moments and the simple joy of being young, where our biggest concerns were every day plans and adventures. This period of my life was characterized by a sense of invincibility and boundless freedom, a time when the future felt like an open road with no visible end. Our days were filled with laughter, exploration, and the easy camaraderie of close friends and family. It was an era of innocence and excitement, where the complexities of adult life were distant shadows on the horizon.

Yet, beneath this surface of ease and excitement, a subtle yet powerful shift was taking place—one that only I could sense. Growing up surrounded by familiar faces, it was easy to overlook the deep changes stirring within me.

Alice, my cousin, was a constant in my world. We shared countless moments of laughter and joy, our connection a blend of ease and affection. Yet, as time progressed, I began to experience a jolt of excitement whenever she was close. It wasn't just her presence; it was the thrill that surged through me, the heart-pounding anticipation that made me acutely aware of her in a way I hadn't before.

The air around Alice was always charged with an undeniable energy. Every glance she cast my way, every casual brush of her hand, seemed to send a jolt through my entire being. It was as if the very atmosphere around us crackled with a vibrant intensity whenever she was near. At first, I tried to dismiss it as just an attraction or a passing infatuation, but the feeling only grew stronger with each interaction. The simple act of her entering a room could shift my focus entirely, as if she were the center of gravity that everything else revolved around.

In those moments, it became clear that I was falling for her, and the realization was both exhilarating and terrifying. Her presence was a constant, electrifying reminder of the connection that was blossoming between us, a connection that was becoming impossible to ignore. Each shared smile, each conversation, felt like a spark igniting something deeper, something that I knew could either light up my world or consume me entirely.

This realization was a personal revelation, an electrifying awakening that I kept hidden within myself. While Alice remained blissfully unaware, treating me with the same warmth and kindness as always, my feelings were evolving into something much deeper. Each encounter with her brought a fresh rush of emotions—an exhilarating sense of possibility and longing that was just mine.

At first, I brushed it aside, dismissing it as just another fleeting infatuation, the kind that comes and goes with the seasons of youth. But the feeling persisted, growing stronger with each passing day. I found myself drawn to her in ways I hadn't anticipated, my thoughts lingering on her long after we had parted ways. It was a one-sided affair, a secret I kept even from myself for the longest time, too unsure and inexperienced to fully grasp the depth of what I was feeling.

But as time went on, that quiet realization began to solidify into something more. It was as if the universe, in its mysterious way, had set things in motion long before I was aware of it. The connection I felt with Alice, though never spoken, had a way of weaving itself into the fabric of my life, subtly influencing the choices I made and the paths I followed.

The excitement of these newfound feelings was undeniable, a vibrant force that was reshaping my perspective. It was as if the simplicity of our childhood was being replaced by a complex, thrilling dance of emotions, setting the stage for a journey that was both exhilarating and uncertain.

For me, this was the beginning of something profound, an emotional adventure that I was only starting to navigate.

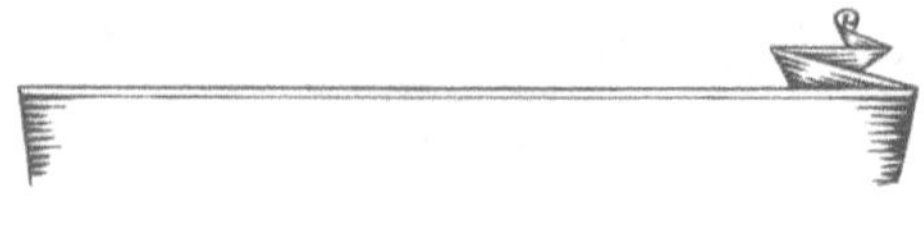

The Marriage

Youth is a time of boundless energy and unbridled optimism, where the world feels vast and full of possibilities. In those early years, life is often a thrilling adventure, each day brimming with new experiences and the promise of something extraordinary just around the corner. There's a certain freedom that comes with being young—a freedom to dream without limits, to pursue passions with relentless enthusiasm, and to navigate the world with a sense of invincibility. The concerns of the future seem distant, and the burdens of responsibility are yet to fully settle on your shoulders.

In those days, life was like a wide-open road, and I was speeding down it without a care in the world. My youth was marked by spontaneity and a carefree attitude, where each moment was lived in the present, with little thought to the consequences. It was a time when emotions ran high and the heart ruled over the head, when friendships were forged in the fires of shared experiences, and love seemed like an intoxicating mystery waiting to be unraveled.

I reveled in the excitement of it all—late nights spent with friends, exploring the city, and indulging in the simple joys of being young. The future, with all its uncertainties, was a distant horizon that I felt no need to worry about. Instead, I was focused on the here and now, soaking up every moment of my youth as if it would last forever.

One morning, when I woke up late as usual, began like any other, a typical start to a day during my early university years—my head filled with the usual thoughts of friends, gatherings, and the carefree musings of youth. I had just started to navigate the complexities of adulthood, and the last thing on my mind was the prospect of marriage. Little did I know, my life was about to take a turn I could never have anticipated.

My parents entered my room with an unusual expression, a blend of seriousness and excitement that immediately pulled me from my routine thoughts. My father, his voice steady yet filled with a subtle undertone of emotion, explained that my grandmother had a heartfelt wish—she wanted me to marry Alice. The name itself stirred something deep within me, a mix of shock, excitement, and disbelief. Alice, the girl who had unknowingly held a place in my heart for so long, was now being presented to me not as a distant dream, but as a real possibility.

I was in my early years of university, barely at the start of my journey into adulthood, and certainly not in a position to support a family. The idea of marriage seemed daunting. But as I sat there, grappling with the enormity of the situation, a sense of excitement began to build within me. This was a dream coming true in the most unexpected way. My father must have seen the conflict in my eyes, for he quickly assured me that he would take care of everything until I was ready to stand on my own.

That reassurance gave me the confidence I needed. I've always had a tendency to embrace the unexpected, to dive headfirst into situations just to see how they unfold. And so, driven by a mix of curiosity, excitement, and the desire to see the surprise on everyone's faces, I agreed. I wanted to see how the world around me would react to this sudden, drastic shift in my life.

I was eager to see how people would react, but amid the excitement, a concern began to grow in the back of my mind. Did Alice feel the same way, or was she being swept along by forces beyond her control? When I asked her, she seemed just as surprised as I was, unsure of what to do or say. In the end, she left the decision to her mother, letting the weight of the moment pull the two of us forward, uncertain but unable to stop what was already in motion.

What followed was a whirlwind. From the moment my parents spoke to me until the moment Alice and I were pronounced husband and wife, a mere 14 hours had passed. It was astonishingly fast, a rapid sequence of events that left everyone, including me, breathless. We shattered the norms, bypassed the usual formalities, and leaped straight into a reality that felt both surreal and exhilarating. That day, amidst the celebrations of Eid, with the entire family gathered, I stood beside Alice, still trying to wrap my mind around how swiftly my life had changed. The speed of it all only added to the dreamlike quality of the experience, leaving me to wonder if any of it was real.

My grandmother's wish for me to marry Alice wasn't just a simple request—it felt like fate stepping in, weaving together my untold feelings with a stroke of luck. The marriage seemed so sudden, almost as if destiny itself had taken the reins, guiding me toward a dream I had never fully voiced.

It was as if the universe had conspired in my favor, aligning every circumstance so that this quiet, long-held desire could finally become reality. But it wasn't just about luck; it was a deeper connection between what I had always wanted and what was meant to be. My grandmother's wish became the catalyst, bringing those hidden emotions to the surface and merging my silent hopes with the path I was destined to walk.

Our marriage wasn't just a union of two people; it was the culmination of a lifetime of unspoken feelings and the beginning of a journey that would shape my understanding of love, commitment, and the sacrifices that come with both. It taught me that love, while beautiful, is also unpredictable and often requires navigating through unexpected challenges. And in those early days, with Alice by my side, I began to realize that love was not just about fulfilling dreams, but about facing the reality that comes with them.

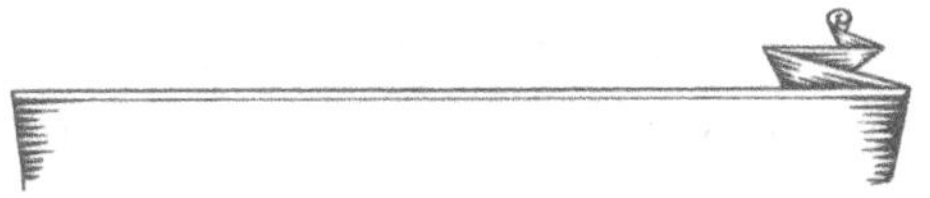

The First Night Together

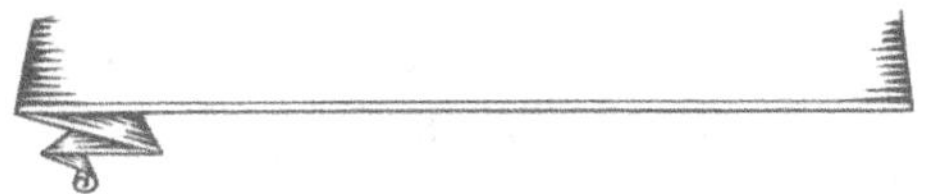

The day of marriage had been a whirlwind—a sudden, intense storm that swept through our lives, leaving us standing together, bound by vows we hadn't anticipated making just hours before. The Eid celebrations had barely ended, and here we were, alone in a room that now symbolized the beginning of our lives as one. The air was thick with a mix of excitement, tension, and the lingering scent of the evening's festivities.

The first night with Alice is a memory that remains vivid, etched in my mind like a perfect painting. She looked breathtaking, a vision of elegance and beauty that left me utterly captivated. Her long, dark hair cascaded over her shoulders, framing a face that was both delicate and striking. The subtle glow of the room's soft lighting only enhanced her natural radiance, highlighting the smoothness of her skin and the gentle curve of her features.

Her earrings, delicate drops that caught the light with every movement, added a touch of grace to her already stunning appearance. But it was her nose ring that truly drew my attention, a simple yet elegant adornment that seemed to perfectly capture her essence—traditional yet with a touch of the unexpected. It was these little details that made her beauty so mesmerizing, the way she carried herself with a quiet confidence that was both alluring and comforting.

Her eyes, large and expressive, held a depth that I found myself lost in. They spoke of emotions that words could never fully capture, a mix of shyness, curiosity, and something unspoken that passed between us. The sari she wore, a deep shade of red with intricate golden embroidery, clung to her in all the right ways. She moved with a grace that seemed almost otherworldly, each step measured, and each gesture soft and deliberate.

As I stood there, taking in the sight of her, I was overwhelmed by a sense of awe and admiration. Alice was more than just beautiful—she was captivating in a way that made everything else fade into the background. That night, her beauty was not just about how she looked but about how she made me feel. It was a beauty that spoke to the soul, a beauty that promised something profound and unforgettable.

I stood there, watching Alice as she sat quietly at the edge of the bed. The soft light from the lamp cast delicate shadows across her face, highlighting the uncertainty in her eyes. My heart pounded with the weight of the moment, a powerful blend of anticipation and a deep, unspoken longing. This was the woman I had silently adored for so long, and now she was my wife. Yet, as I looked at her, I realized that the path to winning her heart was just beginning.

Breaking the silence that hung heavily between us, I asked, my voice carrying the intensity of my emotions, "Alice, do you love me?" It was a question that held the weight of my dreams, my deepest desires, and the future I envisioned for us.

She lifted her gaze to meet mine, and in her eyes, I saw a flicker of confusion, uncertainty, and perhaps even fear. "I'm not sure," she whispered, her voice trembling. "I don't know what love really is."

Her words struck me like a jolt of cold reality, but instead of letting doubt or disappointment take hold, I felt a surge of determination. I had always been a dreamer, a believer in the power of love and the magic it could bring. In that moment, I knew that this was my chance—my chance to show her, to guide her, to help her discover what love truly meant.

"Alice," I said, my voice firm, yet laced with the tenderness I felt for her, "love isn't just a feeling that appears out of nowhere. It's something we build, something we create together. We're at the beginning of a journey—one that will take time, patience, and trust. But I promise you, as we walk this path together, you'll understand. You'll feel it."

I moved closer, sitting beside her, taking her hand in mine. Her skin was soft, her touch tentative, but I held on, offering the strength I hoped would reassure her. "We're young, Alice," I continued, my words filled with the fire of my belief in us. "We have our whole lives ahead of us. And I know, deep down, that love will grow between us, stronger with each passing day."

She looked at me, the uncertainty in her eyes slowly giving way to a glimmer of hope. I could see the struggle within her—trying to reconcile the whirlwind of the day with the new reality we found ourselves in. But I was resolute. I knew that love wasn't just about passion and instant connection; it was about commitment, about choosing to stand by each other, no matter the doubts or fears.

"We'll discover it together," I said, my voice now a whisper, but carrying the full weight of my conviction. "I'm here, and I'm not going anywhere. We don't need to have all the answers right now. What matters is that we're in this together, and I'm going to make sure that you never feel alone on this journey."

Her lips trembled as they curved into a faint, yet genuine smile. The tension between us began to dissolve, replaced by a fragile sense of understanding. It wasn't the fairy tale I had imagined, but it was real, and it was ours.

That night, as we sat together in the quiet of our new reality, I knew that this was the beginning of something profound. Our love story wasn't going to be simple, but it would be strong—because I would make it so. And as we began this journey together, I was determined to show her that love, true love, was worth every moment of doubt, every challenge, and every step we took together. I didn't know how, but I was sure to make things work in a magical way trusting the wonders of fate I had just experienced.

But there was also an unspoken tension, hesitancy in our interactions. We were both aware that while we were now bound by marriage, love had yet to fully take root. It was in the quiet moments, when the conversation would lull, or when our eyes would meet across the room, that I felt the weight of it. I was eager to bridge that gap, to see the seeds of love begin to sprout in the fertile ground of our shared experiences.

Despite the uncertainty, I remained hopeful. Each day was an opportunity to grow closer, to chip away at the walls of formality that still stood between us. And so, with a mix of patience and persistence, I resolved to give her space, yet stay close, to be her constant, but not her burden. The journey of love we had embarked on was just beginning, and I was ready to see where it would lead us.

Love in the Everyday Moments

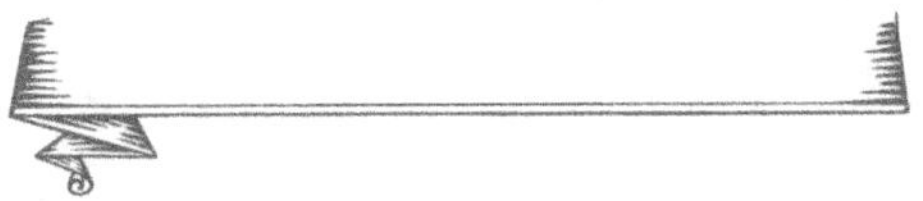

The days following our wedding were nothing short of transcendent, as if the universe had conspired to weave our lives into an epic love story. What began as a cautious bond quickly ignited into an all-consuming passion. Alice, who once seemed uncertain about the very nature of love, was soon enveloped in it, just as I was. Our hearts didn't just sync—they surged, pulsing in rhythm with every shared moment.

Love with Alice wasn't just in the grand gestures or the magical moments; it was in the small, everyday things that made our bond so special. It was in the way we'd steal glances at each other while grocery shopping, turning a mundane task into something intimate and meaningful. It was in the quiet moments at home, where the world seemed to pause as we sipped coffee together in comfortable silence, the unspoken connection between us speaking louder than words ever could.

Everyday life with Alice was like a series of small but significant brushstrokes on the canvas of our relationship, each one adding depth and color to the picture of our love. These simple, shared experiences were what made our bond so profound, grounding us in the reality of our lives together while simultaneously elevating our connection to something extraordinary.

Our life together was a constant stream of love, laughter, and joy. Alice and I found delight in the simplest of things—whether it was a shared meal, a quiet evening walk, or a spontaneous joke that had us both in stitches. Our home was filled with warmth that made even the mundane moments feel special. There was a rhythm to our days, a harmony that came from being so in sync with one another. We reveled in each other's company, finding endless reasons to smile and laugh, making every day feel like a celebration of the love we shared.

At home, our routine was like a silent, yet powerful symphony of love. Mornings often began with quiet moments on the balcony, where we'd sip coffee together as the sun rose, casting a golden hue over everything. We didn't always need to talk; just being there, side by side, was enough. The warmth of the cup in my hands, the cool breeze, and Alice's presence—it was these moments that grounded me, made me feel at peace.

And then there were the evenings, often spent curled up on the couch, with the soft glow of the television casting shadows in the room. We would lose ourselves in movies, but more than that, we lost ourselves in each other's company. Her laughter at a comedy or the way she'd cling to me during a suspenseful scene—it was in these small, quiet moments that I realized just how much she meant to me. The world outside could be chaotic, but in those hours, it was just us, safe in our little cocoon of warmth and affection.

These everyday moments with Alice were like threads that wove our lives together. They might have seemed insignificant to an outsider, but to us, they were everything. Each moment, whether it was as simple as sharing a meal or as intense as a workout, added a new layer to our relationship, making it richer, deeper, and more meaningful. These were the moments that made me realize how truly special our love was—not because of its intensity or passion, but because of its presence in every aspect of our lives. Alice didn't just fill the big gaps in my life; she filled the little spaces too, making our love not just something we felt, but something we lived every single day.

Edward's Birth

Amidst the whirlwind of daily joys and the enchanting routine of our early married life, the thought of parenthood began to gently weave its way into our conversations. The dreams of a shared future, our laughter-filled days, and those moments of pure togetherness made the idea of starting a family increasingly appealing. We found ourselves often drifting into daydreams about a new chapter, one filled with the excitement and challenge of nurturing a life we had created together.

When the news finally came, it was as if our whole world had been illuminated by a new, brilliant light. The prospect of becoming parents was electrifying, transforming our lives from a beautifully crafted dream into a tangible reality. The anticipation of meeting our child filled us with an indescribable joy and a sense of purpose that was both exhilarating and overwhelming.

As Edward's birth approached, the anticipation grew more intense. The night before his arrival, and for three nights afterward, I found myself unable to sleep. My mind was a tempest of emotions—excitement, joy, and a profound sense of responsibility. The thought of holding my newborn son, of seeing him for the first time, was so exhilarating that sleep seemed a distant luxury. Each moment of wakefulness was filled with anticipation, and my thoughts raced with the wonder of what lay ahead. I vividly remember pacing the floor, feeling a mix of nervous energy and uncontainable joy, as I awaited the arrival of our little one.

When Edward finally made his entrance into the world, the experience was nothing short of breathtaking. Holding him for the first time was a moment of indescribable joy, a moment that felt both surreal and incredibly real. His tiny body, so delicate and warm against my chest, was a marvel of creation. Each tiny breath he took seemed to be a testament to the beauty and fragility of life. The sheer wonder of his first cries and the tender touch of his tiny fingers grasping mine were unforgettable.

Watching Edward grow each day was a treasure unlike any other. From the way his tiny hand clung to my finger as he slept on my arm, to the tender moments of making his feeders and pampering him with all the love a father could give—every detail of his early years remains etched in my heart. The joy of buying those tiny shoes, too small to fully capture the enormity of the love I felt, filled our days with a happiness that was beyond words. Every step he took, every laugh, and every sleepy cuddle on my arm was a reminder of the purest love, one that only a parent can understand.

Edward's arrival transformed our lives in ways we had only imagined. Every small detail of those early days was a revelation, from the soft sighs of his sleeping form to the gentle way his eyes would open and explore the world around him. Watching him grow and change, from those first tentative smiles to his first steps, was a journey filled with profound joy and a deep sense of accomplishment. His presence enriched our lives and deepened our love for each other, making every challenge and every triumph a shared experience.

The birth of Edward was not just the beginning of a new chapter; it was a testament to the love that had brought us together and the new life we had created. It was a beautiful reminder of the extraordinary depth of our connection and the boundless joy that comes from welcoming a new life into the world.

The Divorce

As the years passed, the arrival of Edward continued to be a bright spot in our lives. His presence was a constant reminder of the love and joy that had initially brought Alice and me together. The moments we shared as a family were infused with a warmth and connection that seemed to transcend the ordinary, reinforcing the magical sense of our life together.

However, as our lives unfolded, not all was destined to remain as perfect as the fairy tale we had envisioned. Despite the joy that Edward's birth brought into our lives, our journey together faced unforeseen challenges. The initial bliss and the seemingly unbreakable bond we shared began to fray under the weight of external pressures and internal conflicts.

Family interventions, societal expectations, and the relentless force of life's trials began to cast shadows over the radiant days of our early marriage. The magic that once seemed boundless now faced the harsh reality of life's unpredictability. As these pressures mounted, the once-unshakable foundation of our relationship started to crack. The very love that had once felt so complete and perfect was now being tested in ways we hadn't anticipated.

When it all came to an end, I felt shattered, like a glass of wine crushed in the hand. The image of our once-perfect life now lay in fragments, each piece a painful reminder of what we had lost. The heartache was profound, leaving me feeling as though my very essence had been broken, unable to piece together the fragments of my former self.

Neither Alice nor I could pinpoint exactly why our paths diverged so dramatically. We were left with unanswered questions, trying to make sense of how something so beautiful could unravel. This uncertainty added another layer of pain, as we both grappled with the lack of clear reasons behind the separation. It was a stark contrast to the clear and unblemished vision we once held of our future together.

Through this experience, I came to realize that love is not merely about the joy and enchantment of early days. It is also about navigating the hardships and heartaches that come with it. Love can be a force so powerful and overwhelming that it can feel as though it might destroy you. The intense emotions and the depth of our connection revealed that love encompasses, both, the light and the darkness, the highs and the lows. It is not always a fairy tale, but a complex and often painful journey that can leave a lasting impact on one's soul.

In the end, the story of Alice and Me, and of our journey together, is a poignant reminder of how love, in all its forms, shapes and defines our lives, even when its course takes unexpected turns. The memories of those early days, filled with joy, love, and the promise of a future together, remain a cherished part of our story. They serve as a testament to the depth of our connection and the beauty that can emerge from even the most challenging of circumstances.

The Aftermath

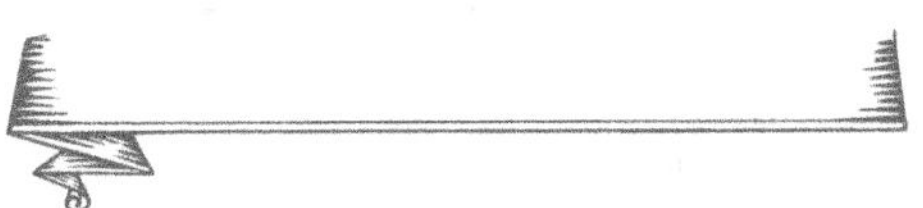

As the reality of our separation took hold, I faced the stark aftermath of a love that once felt like it was destined to endure forever. The vivid memories of our early days, the dreams we had so intricately woven together, and the life we had painstakingly built—each now felt like a haunting echo, gradually dissolving into the emptiness that now stretched between us. The once-bright tapestry of our shared moments was now overshadowed by an overwhelming silence, a void that magnified the weight of our fractured reality.

There was a time when certain songs were the soundtrack of our happiest moments together. Each melody would evoke memories of laughter, late-night drives, and the warmth of her presence beside me. But after the divorce, those same songs took on a different tone. What once brought a smile now triggered a deep, unsettling ache. The melodies that once symbolized togetherness became a reminder of what was lost. Each note seemed to unravel emotions I had tried so hard to keep in check, making it almost impossible to listen without feeling the weight of our separation. The music that had once been a refuge became a mirror, reflecting the void left in the wake of our broken bond.

Love, I came to realize, isn't always the fairytale we envision. It can lift you to the highest peaks of joy, only to plunge you into the deepest chasms of despair. It's an unpredictable storm that doesn't simply end when the rain stops; its aftermath lingers, reshaping the landscape of your heart in ways you never anticipated.

Our separation felt like the shattering of glass, but it wasn't just the relationship that had broken—it was my very self. Each piece of my heart that had once been whole was now fragmented, scattered across the ruins of my life. As I tried to gather the fragments, I discovered that something vital was missing. My heart, the core of who I was, seemed to have vanished into the void.

I was left with a profound emptiness, a hollow space where love and hope once resided. It felt as though the essence of who I had been was lost in the process, leaving behind only a shell of the person I once knew. This void was more than just a feeling; it was a stark, silent echo of the love that had once filled every corner of my being.

In those solitary, reflective moments, I came to a harrowing realization: love isn't just about the joy and fulfillment it brings. It's also about the profound pain it can inflict. Love has the power to elevate you to dizzying heights of happiness, but it also wields the ability to shatter you completely, leaving you in an abyss of emptiness. When it ends, it doesn't just leave a void; it creates a chasm so deep that you feel as though your very soul has been torn apart. The scars it leaves are not mere reminders; they are gaping wounds, a constant, agonizing echo of what once was and what could have been. These wounds don't heal easily—they linger, a raw testament to the love that once consumed you and the heartbreak that has irrevocably changed you.

Fragments of Emotion

The night was heavy with silence as I stood on the terrace, the cool breeze whispering secrets of the past. Edward sat beside me, the weight of unspoken words pressing down on us both. His usually bright eyes were clouded with a sorrow that cut through the darkness. I could feel the distance between us, not just in years but in the uncharted emotional terrain we were now navigating.

Edward finally broke the silence, his voice barely above a whisper. "Why did you leave her, Dad?" The question hung in the air, heavy with the innocence of a child trying to make sense of a world that no longer felt safe or certain.

I took a deep breath, searching for the right words, but knowing that nothing I said would be enough. "Sometimes, Edward, situations change," I began, my voice tinged with the regret I carried every day. "And sometimes, love isn't about sticking together."

Edward looked up at me, his eyes searching mine for answers that I didn't have. "But why does it have to hurt so much?" he asked, his voice trembling.

I swallowed hard, feeling the sting of his pain as if it were my own. "Sometimes, the hardest things in life teach us the most important lessons. And soon, you'll understand that love is complicated. It's beautiful, but it's also fragile."

The silence that followed was thick with unspoken thoughts, and just as it began to feel too heavy, Elsa appeared, her bright energy cutting through the somber mood. She approached us with a soft smile, sensing the tension in the air. "Hey," she said, nudging Edward playfully, "we can't stay out here all night moping. It's freezing, and besides, I want to hear what happened next."

"Ah, Elsa, always so curious," I said, ruffling her hair. "What happened next was the recovery period." I continued...

Chapter 2: Isabelle

The Recovery Plan

In the emptiness felt after my divorce with Alice, I began a desperate search to find someone who could fill the space left by her. I hoped that meeting someone new would restore the sense of completeness I had lost. However, this quest proved to be more painful than the loss itself. I engaged in several relationships, each one a desperate attempt at recreating the joy and intimacy I once knew. But it soon became clear that forcing myself to love someone was a futile and agonizing endeavor. No one could replace Alice, nor could they fill the void she left behind. The notion that love could be manufactured or replicated only led to further disillusionment.

The search for a new love revealed a harsh truth: no one could truly fill the space left by someone so irreplaceable. The effort to manufacture or replicate what I had once shared with Alice felt like an exercise in futility. The notion that love could be artificially created or seamlessly transferred was shattered by the reality that such attempts only resulted in more chaos and emptiness.

In the midst of this emotional turmoil, with each relationship failing to bridge the gap left behind, a sense of despair began to settle in. Everything seemed to be falling apart, leaving me feeling increasingly hollow. It was within this maelstrom of confusion and sorrow that Isabelle entered my life—a presence that, against the backdrop of chaos, offered a glimmer of hope and the possibility of renewal. Her arrival marked a turning point, suggesting that perhaps amidst the wreckage, there was still a chance for something meaningful to emerge.

Isabelle wasn't a potential savior or a replacement for Alice; she was a beacon of calm in my storm. Her insights were not grandiose or prescriptive but carried a quiet depth that resonated with me deeply. She spoke of how life continues to evolve, how the passage of time brings change, and how we must learn to navigate the ebb and flow of our emotions. Her words provided a much-needed perspective, reminding me that healing and growth are part of life's ongoing journey.

All my efforts to find a new love to replace Alice had been futile. Each attempt felt like grasping at shadows, unable to fill the void she left behind. It became clear that no amount of new relationships could replicate what had been lost. What I needed wasn't another love but rather a friend—a true confidant who could help me find my way through the darkness.

Isabelle's presence was a crucial reminder that while the search for new love had been fruitless, the support of a genuine friend was invaluable. Through our conversations, she offered the understanding and calm I needed, showing me that life doesn't end with loss but continues to evolve, offering new opportunities for connection and renewal. It was through this understanding that I began to find a semblance of peace, even as I continued to grapple with the lingering shadows of my past.

Isabelle was a breath of fresh air in a world that had become stifling. She had a gentle way of reminding me that life, in all its complexities and heartaches, continues to evolve. She spoke of how time, though it doesn't erase pain, has a way of softening its edges, allowing space for new growth. Through her words, I began to see that perhaps love wasn't something to be found or forced, but something that might come in its own time, in its own way.

What I had sought in the wrong places—a rekindling of lost love—was never going to bring me peace. What I needed was a friend who could listen without judgment, offer wisdom without preaching, and provide comfort without expectation. Isabelle became that friend.

She was the steady presence I needed, the voice that cut through the noise of my own thoughts and fears. Through her, I began to understand that healing wasn't about finding someone to replace what was lost but about finding a way to live with the loss, to move forward even when it feels impossible.

In Isabelle, I didn't find love in the traditional sense, but I found something just as powerful: a friendship that allowed me to start piecing myself back together. She showed me that sometimes, it's not about searching for what's missing but about learning to live with the emptiness, and in doing so, making room for something new to grow.

The Flicker

Isabelle wasn't just a friend; she was the embodiment of patience and understanding, a rare presence in the tumultuous world I had found myself in. She navigated the storm within me with a grace that felt almost ethereal, gently untangling the twisted knots of pain and despair that had taken root in my heart. Where others had stumbled, unable to grasp the depths of my sorrow, Isabelle remained, steadfast and unwavering, guiding me through the darkest recesses of my soul. Her words were like keys, unlocking doors to the life I thought had slipped away, and in those moments, I felt a sensation I hadn't experienced in what seemed like an eternity—a glimmer of hope.

As she tenderly pieced together the fragments of my shattered heart, something unexpected began to stir within her. Isabelle saw the depth of my love—a love that could lay itself bare, vulnerable and unguarded, even after being broken. She didn't just see the wounded man I had become; she saw the man I once was—the man who had loved with a depth and passion that few could comprehend. And in witnessing that, Isabelle found herself drawn to me in ways she hadn't anticipated.

What began as a fleeting flicker—a passing warmth she quickly dismissed—soon grew into a steady flame that illuminated corners of her heart she hadn't known existed. Isabelle began to see me not merely as the friend she was helping to heal, but as someone she could genuinely love—a love that felt as tender as it was powerful, as surprising as it was inevitable.

Isabelle's heart began to craft a narrative of its own, a story where we weren't just two souls seeking comfort in each other's company, but two hearts destined to intertwine, like stars finding their place in a perfect constellation. She envisioned a future where the love that once belonged to Alice could be reborn—not as a shadow of the past, but as the dawn of something new and profoundly beautiful.

This newfound love wasn't a replacement or a remedy; it was a new chapter, a possibility she hadn't foreseen but one that felt undeniably right. In her heart, we became more than just friends; we became two people whose paths had converged for reasons that felt like destiny. She imagined a future where love could flourish again, where we could build something unique and enduring together.

As these feelings blossomed within her, they brought a mix of joy and apprehension. Isabelle knew that love, true love, wasn't something to be hurried or forced. Yet, the connection she felt with me was undeniable, and with each passing day, she found herself more deeply enmeshed in emotions she hadn't expected—emotions that were as exhilarating as they were terrifying.

As the months passed, our friendship deepened, becoming an anchor in the storm that was my life. Isabelle was the steady force I clung to, her presence a source of comfort and solace amidst the chaos left by Alice. Yet, beneath the surface of our conversations, an unspoken tension simmered—a quiet, growing awareness that our bond was evolving into something more profound.

Our late-night talks grew longer, filled with silences that spoke louder than words. In those moments, I could feel something changing, something neither of us had the courage to name. Isabelle, with her compassionate understanding, seemed to sense it too. She had seen me at my lowest, had helped piece together the fragments of my shattered self, and in doing so, had unknowingly found a place in my heart that I hadn't realized was still open.

But with this new closeness came a creeping fear, a doubt that gnawed at the edges of our burgeoning connection. Could this really be love, or was it just a desperate attempt to fill the void Alice had left behind? Were we falling for each other, or were we simply reaching out for comfort in a world that suddenly felt too vast and empty?

Isabelle, ever patient and gentle, didn't push. She let our relationship unfold naturally, allowing time to reveal the true nature of our feelings. Yet, with every passing day, the line between friendship and something more blurred, making it harder to distinguish where one ended and the other began.

One quiet evening, as we spoke in the hushed tones of two people who had shared everything but their deepest fears, Isabelle finally broke the silence that had been growing between us. With a mix of hesitation and hope, she confessed the feelings that had been building within her, feelings that had taken root in the fertile ground of our shared pain and mutual understanding.

As I listened to her words, a tidal wave of emotions crashed over me. My heart, still bruised and fragile from the past, struggled to process the depth of her feelings. I was confronted with a painful truth: while Isabelle had been my beacon in the darkness, a part of me had also been quietly falling for her. But as a broken soul, I was paralyzed by fear and uncertainty. Even though I sensed a burgeoning affection within myself, I lacked the courage to fully acknowledge it. I was overwhelmed by the fear of hurting her, especially after she had been my unwavering support through my worst moments. The thought of revealing my own vulnerabilities and feelings seemed almost too risky, as if admitting them would shatter the fragile trust we had built. My heart was still in pieces from the past, and the prospect of entering a new relationship felt like stepping into the unknown. I feared that my own brokenness might hurt her, that my inability to fully commit might cause her pain. So, instead of embracing the possibility of a new beginning, I remained silent, grappling with the fear that I might not be strong enough to pursue a deeper connection. Yet, beneath the surface of my hesitation, there was a glimmer of hope—a hope that maybe, just maybe, what we shared could grow into something beautiful and healing. But the fear of failure and the weight of my past made it difficult to see a clear path forward. As Isabelle's words hung in the air, I was left to wrestle with my own fears and the delicate balance between wanting to protect her and acknowledging the feelings that were slowly, hesitantly, emerging within me.

But in that moment of uncertainty, I realized something crucial: the journey to love, even when fraught with fear and hesitation, is also a path to self-discovery. Perhaps the very act of confronting my fears and embracing vulnerability was the key to unlocking a future I had almost given up on.

With Isabelle's sincerity laid bare before me, I faced the profound truth that love, in all its complexity, required not just courage but also an open heart willing to take risks. And as I stood on the precipice of this new beginning, I knew that the choice to embrace or retreat would define not only our future but also my own journey toward healing and growth.

The road ahead was uncertain, and the scars of the past still ached, but for the first time in a long while, I felt a glimmer of possibility—an invitation to step into the unknown and see where this new chapter might lead.

The Dawn of New Beginnings

As I grappled with the whirlwind of emotions stirred by Isabelle's confession, our relationship entered a new phase. What had once been a comforting friendship began to shift, revealing the potential for something deeper and more profound.

Isabelle's presence became a source of solace and excitement. Our conversations grew more intimate, and moments that had once been casual now carried an undercurrent of unspoken understanding. We found ourselves sharing more than just our daily lives; we began to confide in each other about our dreams, fears, and the struggles that had shaped us. Through this deepening connection, I began to see Isabelle not just as a friend but as someone who could possibly help mend the broken pieces of my heart.

Despite the growing affection, I remained cautious. My past experiences had taught me the fragility of love, and I was reluctant to fully open myself up again. Isabelle was patient and kind, allowing me to take my time, and this grace became a foundation upon which we could build. She did not demand answers or rush me into anything but rather gave me the space to navigate my feelings at my own pace.

Our shared moments began to carry a new significance. The laughter we shared, the quiet evenings spent together, and the comfort of simply being in each other's company started to feel like pieces of a puzzle falling into place. Yet, beneath the surface, I struggled with the fear that my own uncertainties might cloud the potential for something beautiful.

Isabelle's unwavering support and understanding helped bridge the gap between my past wounds and the possibility of a future together. I started to see our relationship as a journey—one where both of us were navigating our way through the remnants of our pasts toward something new and hopeful.

But as our bond deepened, so did my internal struggle. The fear of vulnerability and the burden of past scars still lingered, casting shadows over the bright prospects of our future. It was clear that our journey together would require not only patience and understanding but also the courage to face the uncertainties that lay ahead.

As time went by, Isabelle and I grew closer, our friendship transforming into something deeper than either of us had anticipated. She had been the rock I needed, offering support, wisdom, and a kind of quiet strength that felt like a salve to the wounds left by my past. Our connection began in the most ordinary way, through messages and conversations that carried an undercurrent of warmth and understanding, but it didn't stay that way for long.

I often confided in Isabelle, laying bare the remnants of my brokenness—the confusion, the pain, and the shattered pieces of my heart. She listened without judgment, her presence a soothing constant, and slowly, I found myself relying on her more and more. In her, I saw a gentle but powerful spirit, someone who had the capacity to understand the complexity of my emotions without expecting me to be more than I could be at the time. I needed her in a way that I hadn't realized before, not as a lover but as a friend who could hold me together when I felt like falling apart.

Every moment spent talking to her took away the weightage of the burden I once thought would accompany me for the rest of my life. Weaving our dreams together felt like a new beginning with ever soothing possibilities ahead. This relation was so special that putting a name to it would be injustice to the very essence of it.

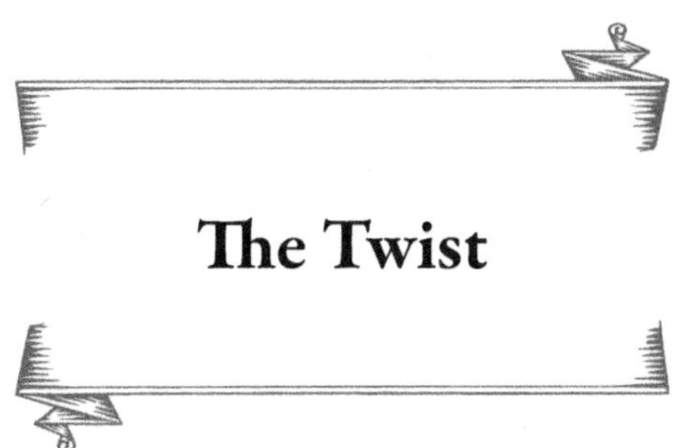

The Twist

Isabelle's selflessness was something that struck me deeply. She never asked for anything in return for the comfort and solace she provided. She simply listened, understood, and stayed by my side, even when the weight of my past threatened to overwhelm me. She saw the broken pieces of my heart, the fragments that I struggled to put back together, and without hesitation, she took it upon herself to help me heal.

But as these dreams began to take shape, the reality of what Isabelle would have to give up for them started to weigh heavily on my heart. Isabelle was not just a kind soul; she was a woman of immense potential, with dreams and aspirations that were uniquely her own. She had a path she was meant to follow, ambitions that she had worked tirelessly to achieve, and an identity that was deeply rooted in her experiences, beliefs, and desires.

Choosing a life with me would mean sacrificing many of those things. She would have to leave behind certain dreams that she had nurtured for years, dreams that defined who she was and who she wanted to become. The career she had worked so hard to build, the independence she had fiercely protected, and the personal goals she had set for herself—all of these would be compromised if she chose to align her life with mine.

Moreover, the love she offered was not without its cost. Isabelle was prepared to step into a life that was far from uncomplicated. She was willing to bear the weight of my past, to accept the challenges that came with loving someone as scarred as I was. She was ready to navigate the complexities of my emotional landscape, to endure the shadows of my previous relationships, and to face the uncertain future we might have together. But what haunted me the most was the realization that, in choosing this life with me, Isabelle would lose a part of herself.

The Isabelle I had come to know was fiercely independent, with a vibrant spirit that was both captivating and inspiring. She was a woman who knew her worth, who valued her freedom and autonomy, and who had a clear vision of the life she wanted to lead. To ask her to give up even a fraction of that for me felt like a crime, an act of selfishness that I couldn't reconcile with my conscience.

I knew that if we pursued this path, Isabelle would be forced to make sacrifices that would alter the course of her life forever. She would have to put aside her own desires, to reshape her identity to fit into the mold of a life that was centered upon my needs, my wounds, and my past. The very things that made her unique—the passions, the dreams, the goals she had set for herself—would be eclipsed by the demands of a relationship that required her to prioritize me above herself.

This realization struck me with a force that I hadn't anticipated. The burden of knowing that Isabelle was willing to give up so much for me became almost unbearable. How could I allow her to lose the essence of who she was? How could I let her sacrifice the very things that made her the incredible person I had come to care for so deeply?

Isabelle's love was a gift, but it was also a reminder of the cost that comes with deep emotional connections. As much as I wanted to embrace the future we had envisioned, I couldn't ignore the fact that her sacrifices would come at a great personal cost. The dreams we had spun together, as beautiful as they were, began to feel like a weight on my heart—a weight that grew heavier with each passing day.

In the end, the burden of her potential sacrifices became too much for me to bear. I couldn't let her give up so much of herself for my sake. The love she offered was pure and unconditional, but it was also a love that demanded more from her than I was willing to take. As much as I wanted to hold on to the life we had imagined, I knew that I couldn't allow her to lose herself in the process.

And so, I found myself at a crossroads, torn between the desire to build a life with Isabelle and the realization that doing so would mean asking her to give up too much. It was a painful truth to confront, but it was one that I couldn't ignore. Isabelle deserved to live her life fully, to chase her dreams without restraint, and to be the person she was meant to be. As much as it hurt to acknowledge, I knew that I couldn't let my love for her become a cage that held her back from all that she could achieve.

After days of wrestling with the weight of Isabelle's potential sacrifices, I knew I couldn't keep these thoughts to myself any longer. The visions of our future, once so bright and hopeful, had become clouded with the harsh realities I could no longer ignore. I cared too much for Isabelle to let her walk into something that might cause her pain down the line, and as difficult as it was, I needed to be honest with her.

One evening I gathered the courage to voice the concerns that had been haunting me. "Isabelle," I began my voice heavy with emotion, "I need to talk to you about something that's been on my mind." I took a deep breath and continued, "I've been thinking a lot about the future, about everything we've been planning. And I can't shake the feeling that you're giving up too much for me."

She started to protest, but I gently raised my hand to stop her. "Please, just hear me out," I said softly. "You have so many dreams, so much potential, and I'm afraid that by choosing to be with me, you'll be sacrificing the things that make you who you are."

I could see the confusion and hurt beginning to surface at her side, but I pressed on. "Life with me isn't going to be the fairytale we've imagined. It's going to be a roller coaster ride, full of challenges and troubles. I'm still trying to pick up the pieces of my past, and I don't know if I'm strong enough to give you the life you deserve."

The words were difficult to say, each one feeling like a sharp blade cutting into my own heart. But I needed her to understand the reality of what we were facing. "Reality," I continued, "isn't as beautiful as our imaginations. The dreams we've shared are wonderful, but they're just that—dreams. The truth is, life together won't be easy. There will be times when it feels like everything is falling apart, when the weight of the past becomes too much to bear. And I'm terrified that one day, you'll look back and regret giving up so much for someone who might not be able to give you the happiness you deserve.

Isabelle's eyes glistened with unshed tears, and I could see the pain my words were causing her. But I knew that this was the most loving thing I could do for her—to be honest, even if it hurt. "You've been so selfless, so giving," I said, my voice breaking, "but I can't let you lose yourself for me. You deserve to chase your dreams, to live a life that's full and fulfilling, without the burden of my brokenness weighing you down."

The silence that followed was almost unbearable. I could see the internal struggle in her eyes, the battle between her love for me and the reality I had just laid out before her. I wanted so badly to tell her that everything would be okay, that we could make it work, but I knew that wouldn't be fair to her. The truth was, I was scared—scared of the future, scared of hurting her, and scared of the possibility that I might not be able to love her in the way she deserved.

Finally, Isabelle spoke, her voice trembling with emotion. "I don't care about the challenges, about the difficulties. I care about you," she said, her eyes pleading with me to see things from her perspective. "I'm not afraid of the struggles, because I believe that together, we can overcome them."

Her words were like a lifeline to a drowning man, offering hope and warmth. Yet, even as they reached out to me, I couldn't ignore the doubts that gnawed at my conscience. "But what if you do regret it one day?" I asked, my voice barely above a whisper. "What if you wake up and realize that you've given up too much, that you've lost yourself in the process?"

She shook her head, tears now streaming down her face. "I know what I'm choosing, and I'm choosing you," she said firmly. "But if you truly believe that I'll regret it, if you think that I'm making a mistake, you don't know me at all."

Her words cut deep, piercing through the fragile hopes I had clung to. She was willing to give everything for us, but I couldn't shake the fear that, in doing so, she would lose herself—the vibrant, independent woman I had come to admire and care for so deeply.

As the days passed, I watched as Isabelle continued to try to make our dreams come true, her determination unwavering. She was relentless in her efforts, pouring herself into every plan, every conversation about our future. But with each step forward, the weight on my shoulders grew heavier. I couldn't help but see the sacrifices she was making, the parts of herself she was willing to set aside for our relationship.

It tore me apart to see her invest so much of herself into a future that I wasn't sure I could give her. I began to distance myself, not out of lack of love, but out of fear—fear that by letting her continue down this path, I was complicit in the slow erosion of her true self. I started to be cold, withdrawing emotionally, hoping that by doing so, I could protect her from the pain I knew was inevitable.

I knew I was hurting her, but I couldn't see any other way to make her understand the reality of what we were facing. I had to make her see that the fairytale we had imagined was just that—a fairytale. And the cost of pursuing it could be the loss of everything that made her the incredible person she was.

In the end, it wasn't my words that made her realize the truth, but the coldness I showed her—the emotional distance that grew between us as I tried to hold her back from what could potentially destroy the essence of who she was. It was the hardest thing I've ever had to do, but I couldn't stand the thought of her losing herself for me.

Our dreams, once so vivid and full of promise, began to fade, not because they weren't possible, but because I couldn't allow her to lose herself in the pursuit of a love that might not have been strong enough to survive the harsh light of reality. The more she tried to cling to those dreams, the more I pulled away, until there was nothing left but the cold, hard truth that we both had to face.

Isabelle deserved more than what I could offer her, and as much as it broke my heart to do it, I had to let her go—not because I didn't love her, but because I loved her too much to let her give up everything for me.

The resistance within me grew so overpowering that I felt I had no choice but to bury every vestige of my feelings, encasing them in a fortress of cold detachment. I became someone I barely recognized—rigid, unfeeling, and harsh. My words, which had once been a source of warmth and comfort, transformed into tools of emotional destruction. I spoke with a deliberate severity; choosing phrases that I knew would hurt Isabelle deeply, all under the guise of protecting her from a future I feared would be fraught with regret and loss.

Yet, in my desperate attempt to shield her from potential pain, I was blind to the depth of the wounds I was inflicting in the present. Every cruel remark, every deliberate act of distancing was a painful cut to the heart of our relationship. My actions were meant to guard her from a hypothetical future, but instead, they drove a brutal wedge between us.

Isabelle, who had been nothing but compassionate, supportive, and selflessly devoted to me, was now subjected to the harshest of my fears and insecurities. She was left grappling with a barrage of emotionally cold behavior and cutting remarks that shattered the trust and connection we had built. In pushing her away, I forced her to endure not only the loss of the dreams we had shared but also the profound hurt of feeling unworthy of the love she had so generously given.

Each calculated distance I created was like a wound to her heart, an attempt to force her to see the potential pitfalls of our future together.

She endured my emotional isolation with a heartbreaking patience, all while her own hopes and feelings were trampled under the weight of my self-protective barriers. Isabelle's love, once a source of healing and connection, was now met with a coldness that left her struggling to reconcile the warmth she had known with the chilling distance I imposed.

In retrospect, the pain I inflicted on Isabelle was a direct consequence of my own fears and doubts. My actions, intended to prevent future regret, only resulted in the immediate, excruciating hurt that she had to bear. Her selflessness and understanding, which had once been the foundation of our connection, were now met with the very coldness I had hoped to shield her from. I had, in my misguided effort to protect her, caused her the kind of pain that left her not only heartbroken but questioning the very love that had once been our greatest solace.

As I wrestled with my fears and insecurities, I felt myself shutting down the very essence of my capacity to love. In my misguided attempt to protect Isabelle from future pain, I made a decision that would ultimately shut her out. I became resolute, almost mechanical in my detachment, convinced that forcing her to accept my decision was the only way to safeguard her from what I believed was a doomed path.

Yet, in my effort to shield her from potential suffering, I inflicted a wound far deeper than any I had endured myself. The harsh reality of my actions became painfully clear: I had not only dismissed my own ability to love but had also shattered Isabelle's heart in the process. The strength of her spirit, which had been so selflessly dedicated to supporting me, was now left broken and scattered by the very person she had sought to help.

The pain I had sought to avoid in our future was now mirrored in the agony that Isabelle felt. Her anguish surpassed my own, a testament to the depth of her feelings and the sacrifice she was willing to make for us. In trying to protect her from a future that might never come to pass, I had destroyed the present, leaving her to grapple with a heartache that was all too real.

The finality of my decision marked a somber end to a chapter filled with unfulfilled dreams and unresolved emotions. I had closed off a part of myself that had once been capable of profound love, and in doing so, had denied Isabelle the future we had both envisioned. The weight of this realization was crushing—a stark reminder of the cost of my own fears and the irrevocable impact of my choices.

As the chapter concluded, I was left to confront the echoes of the pain I had caused, the heartbreak I had unleashed. The journey forward would be one of reckoning with the consequences of my decisions, seeking redemption, and understanding the true cost of trying to control the unpredictability of love.

The Hybrid Approach

In the aftermath of my split with Isabelle, I found myself retreating into a state of emotional coldness. The harshness I had projected onto her became a shield I used to guard myself against further pain. This newfound detachment, though initially a defense mechanism, began to take on a life of its own. I started to relish the distance, finding a perverse comfort in the emotional numbness that had enveloped me.

There was a certain allure in this cold self I had become. It offered a sense of control and predictability in a world that had previously been chaotic and fraught with emotional turmoil. By suppressing my feelings and maintaining a façade of indifference, I convinced myself that I was protecting myself from future heartbreak. I began to embrace this persona, seeing it as a necessary adaptation to shield my fragile heart from the vulnerabilities that had caused me so much suffering.

However, as time passed, the veneer of coldness I had carefully crafted began to feel less like a shield and more like a cage. The realization that, despite my best efforts to remain emotionally detached, I still needed connection and support started to seep in. The isolation I experienced, though self-imposed, began to erode my sense of stability and sanity.

I found myself yearning for human connection, not necessarily for love, but for companionship and understanding. The coldness that once seemed like a sanctuary now felt like a prison, and the need for someone to keep my sanity intact became undeniable. It was clear that no amount of emotional distance could fully replace the comfort and stability that a genuine connection with another person could provide.

Despite this growing awareness, I remained deeply wary of fully opening myself up to love again. The scars from my past experiences, particularly the pain inflicted upon Isabelle, made me hesitant to dive back into the depths of emotional vulnerability. I had convinced myself that while companionship was necessary, I would approach it with extreme caution.

I resolved to engage with others without surrendering my entire self to the prospect of love. I adopted a strategy of keeping relationships at a manageable distance, allowing myself to experience the benefits of connection while avoiding the intensity of full emotional investment. It was a balancing act—remaining open enough to maintain my sanity but guarded enough to protect myself from potential heartache.

In this new approach, I sought to strike a balance between emotional self-preservation and the human need for interaction. I engaged in friendships and connections with a measured openness, allowing myself to enjoy the companionship without falling into the trap of total emotional dependency. This new way of relating to others provided a semblance of stability and satisfaction while keeping my heart at a safe distance from the vulnerabilities that had previously caused me so much pain.

As I navigated this delicate balance, I began to understand that while the cold self I had embraced offered some protection, it was not a perfect solution. It was a temporary measure, a way to cope with the aftermath of past hurts and to navigate the complexities of future relationships. I acknowledged that true emotional fulfillment required a more nuanced approach, one where I could engage with others authentically without sacrificing my own well-being.

Thus, I continued to tread carefully, embracing a cautious optimism for the future. The journey of self-discovery and emotional healing was ongoing, and while I remained vigilant against the risks of love, I also remained open to the possibility that connection could be a source of profound joy and growth. This newfound perspective allowed me to approach relationships with a more balanced and thoughtful mindset, preparing me for whatever lay ahead.

The Closure

As I finish recounting the emotional whirlwind with Isabelle, the night air feels cold, almost as if the coldness of the past is reflecting upon the present. I take a moment, letting the silence stretch, giving everyone a chance to absorb what I've shared. The city hums softly below us, a stark contrast to the turmoil I've just relived.

A voice broke the silence. It was Edward again, his tone thoughtful and slightly bewildered. "Dad, I can't really picture you as the cold, distant person you're describing. You've always been warm with us, always present," he said, his brows furrowed as he tried to reconcile the image of his father with the story I had just shared.

I sighed, a small smile playing on my lips. "I wasn't always this way, Edward. Life... it changes you. But that part of me, the one you've never seen, was very real back then."

Before Edward could respond, Elsa, ever the mischievous one, chimed in with a playful smirk. "So, Dad, what else have you been hiding from us? You always seemed like you had it all together, but I guess there's a lot more beneath the surface, huh?"

Her teasing tone lightened the mood slightly, and I couldn't help but chuckle. "There's a lot I've kept to myself, Elsa. Some things are just too complicated to share until the time is right."

Sophia, the most introspective of the three, had been quietly absorbing everything. She finally spoke up, her voice tinged with curiosity. "But where does Mom fit into all of this? You've talked about these past relationships, but how did you end up with her? What happened after Isabelle?"

Her question hung in the air, charged with an intensity that made me pause. The journey with Sarah was a significant chapter, one that brought both healing and new challenges. But before we could dive into that story, there was more they needed to understand about the path that led me there.

"That's a story for another time," I said, gently evading the full answer for now. "But I promise we'll get there. I just need you to understand how the person I was, shaped the man I am today. Every experience, every mistake, every attempt to shield myself—it all led to where I am now, with your mother and with all of you."

They nodded: a mix of anticipation and understanding in their eyes. The conversation had brought us closer, a small window into the complexities of my past, yet it also left them with more questions—a perfect transition into the next chapter of my story.

I continued...

Chapter 3: Florence

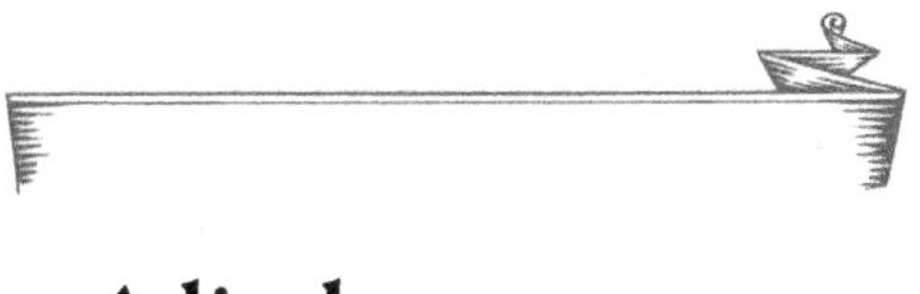

A lively encounter

In the wake of the emotional barricade I had built around myself, a fortress of coldness and detachment, I found a new presence emerging in my world. After my heart-wrenching attempt to shield Isabelle from potential regrets, I had committed myself to a life where emotions were subdued and love was a distant memory. I ventured into new connections, but my interactions were now carefully moderated, devoid of the depth I once craved.

Florence entered my life as just another name in the crowded expanse of online acquaintances, yet she was different from the start. At first glance, she was just another friend in the vast sea of digital acquaintances. But there was something magnetic about her presence. Unlike the subdued interactions I had grown accustomed to, Florence exuded a vibrant energy that was impossible to ignore. Her laughter was infectious, her perspectives on life refreshing.

Florence was a woman of striking beauty, her appearance as captivating as her personality. Her nose had a subtle curve, adding a unique charm to her face. Big, wide eyes, full of life and curiosity, seemed to capture every detail of the world around her. Her long hair, always perfectly maintained with a decent trim, flowed gracefully, framing her face in a way that highlighted her features. There was an effortless elegance about her, a blend of natural beauty and a lively spirit that made her even more of a charming presence.

From our first exchanges, it was evident that Florence possessed an innate charm. Her messages were more than just responses; they were filled with lively anecdotes and a zest for life that was both refreshing and intriguing. She spoke with a kind of animated enthusiasm that was rare in the sea of digital voices I had grown accustomed to. It was clear that Florence wasn't just passing time online; she was truly engaged and passionate about sharing her experiences and thoughts.

What struck me most about Florence was her ability to bring a sense of vitality into our conversations. Her stories of spontaneous trips, vibrant social gatherings, and her unfiltered joy in daily activities were like bursts of color in my otherwise monochrome routine. She had a way of talking about her life that made it sound like an ongoing adventure, one that she embraced with both hands.

As our conversations continued, I found myself looking forward to our interactions more and more. Florence's presence in my life was like a ray of sunshine piercing through a cloudy sky. Her carefree attitude and genuine joy were a stark contrast to the guarded emotional state I had developed. Every interaction with her felt like a small escape from my own complexities, a chance to experience the world through her vibrant lens.

Florence's approach to life and our budding friendship began to gently challenge my own worldview. Her ability to find beauty in ordinary moments and her refusal to be bogged down by the weight of past experiences reminded me of the life I once lived—before the emotional trials had shaped me into a more reserved and cautious person. In Florence, I saw a reflection of a past self I had nearly forgotten, and this connection became a source of both nostalgia and inspiration.

Florence perfectly fit into the hybrid model I had envisioned for myself—a friend who brought vibrancy into my life without the complexities of emotional baggage that often accompanies romantic relationships. Her presence was refreshing and uplifting, serving as a source of joy and perspective. This new model allowed me to enjoy a meaningful and dynamic friendship without risking the entanglements of deep emotional involvement. Florence's approach to life complemented my desire to maintain control over my emotional boundaries while still savoring the benefits of a rich, fulfilling connection.

As our conversations continued, I found myself looking forward to our interactions more and more. Florence's presence in my life was like a ray of sunshine piercing through a cloudy sky. Her carefree attitude and genuine joy were a stark contrast to the guarded emotional state I had developed. Every interaction with her felt like a small escape from my own complexities, a chance to experience the world through her vibrant lens.

As our bond grew, I realized that Florence was more than just a fleeting acquaintance. She represented a beacon of the vibrant life I longed to reconnect with. Yet, as much as I cherished her presence, I knew that preserving the purity of our friendship was crucial. I was determined to keep the relationship within the boundaries of friendship, valuing the emotional refuge and perspective she provided without letting it evolve into something more complicated.

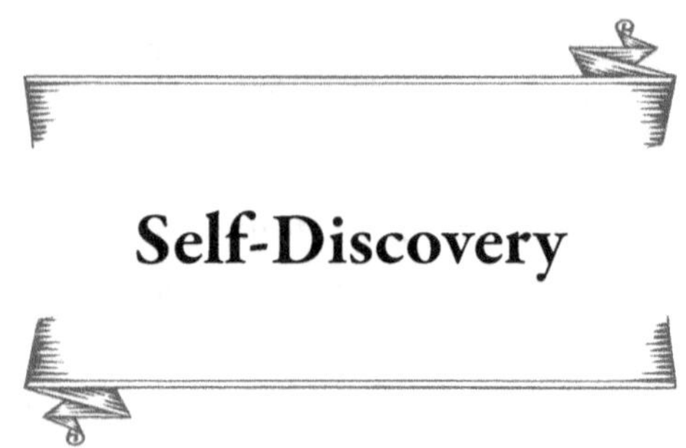

Self-Discovery

Florence's presence in my life catalyzed a profound journey of self-discovery. Her vibrant energy and unique approach to life acted as a lens through which I could reevaluate my own identity and emotional landscape. This period of self-discovery was not just about recognizing who I had become but also about rediscovering parts of myself that had been buried beneath layers of past experiences and emotional turbulence.

Her approach to life was a stark contrast to the cautious, sometimes jaded persona I had adopted after my tumultuous experiences. Through our interactions, I began to peel back the layers of emotional detachment and rediscover the parts of myself that were still capable of genuine happiness and spontaneity. Florence's ability to find delight in everyday moments helped me understand that these qualities were still a part of me, waiting to be reignited.

One of the most enlightening aspects of my time with Florence was the opportunity to reassess my needs and boundaries in relationships. Her friendship provided a safe space to explore emotional connections without the pressures and expectations of romantic involvement. This allowed me to examine what I truly needed from relationships and how to establish healthy boundaries that would enable me to maintain both personal integrity and emotional connection.

Florence's presence taught me the value of emotional balance. I learned that it was possible to engage deeply with someone while still preserving a sense of self. This realization was crucial in understanding how to approach future relationships, including the importance of setting boundaries and managing expectations to ensure that connections were fulfilling without being overwhelming.

Florence's influence also offered valuable insights into the nature of love and relationships. By maintaining a close but non-romantic friendship with her, I experienced a different dimension of emotional connection—one that was characterized by mutual respect, support, and understanding without the complications of romantic attachment. This experience broadened my perspective on love, showing me that it could be both enriching and manageable when approached with clarity and intention.

Through this period of self-discovery, I began to appreciate the nuances of love as a force that could be harnessed and controlled rather than something that needed to consume every aspect of life. Florence's role in my journey emphasized the importance of emotional balance and the power of maintaining a sense of self within relationships.

The insights gained from my interactions with Florence prepared me for future growth and relationships. Her influence helped me understand that self-discovery is an ongoing process and that each relationship offers a chance to learn more about oneself. I entered subsequent relationships with a greater sense of awareness and control, knowing that the lessons learned from my time with Florence had equipped me with the tools to navigate love and connection more effectively.

The Balancing Act

As our conversations deepened, the bond between Florence and me evolved into something that transcended typical online interactions. Our dialogues became a highlight of my day, offering a rare and invigorating glimpse into a world brimming with enthusiasm and joy. Florence had a way of turning mundane topics into vibrant discussions, weaving humor and insights into her narratives. Her words painted vivid pictures of her experiences, making each conversation feel like a shared adventure.

During our exchanges, I found myself reflecting on aspects of my own life I had long overlooked. Florence's stories of spontaneous adventures and her ability to find beauty in everyday moments resonated deeply with me. It was as if she had a magical ability to draw out my own dormant appreciation for life's simpler pleasures. Through her, I began to reawaken a sense of wonder that I had suppressed for years, lost in the complexities of my emotional landscape.

One of the most delightful aspects of our connection was the laughter we shared. Florence's infectious humor and lightheartedness brought a refreshing break from the weighty introspections I often found myself entangled in. Her ability to find joy in the little things was both endearing and uplifting. These moments of shared laughter and lightness were a testament to the genuine and enjoyable nature of our friendship, highlighting the ease and comfort we found in each other's company.

During our time together, there was an underlying flirtation that would surface occasionally. I would throw in a playful comment or a teasing remark, and Florence would respond with a smile, always knowing just how to maintain that delicate balance between being friendly and keeping things respectful. It was this graceful way she handled our interactions that made our connection feel so unique and easygoing.

Florence's vibrant outlook on life began to shift my own perspective. I started to see my own experiences through her eyes—eyes that saw the world as a canvas of opportunities and delights. Her enthusiasm was a catalyst for change, challenging me to reconsider how I approached daily life. It wasn't about changing who I was but rather rediscovering parts of myself that had been overshadowed by past experiences.

As time went on, the friendship with Florence evolved into a unique and cherished part of my life. It wasn't just about enjoying her company; it was about appreciating the positive impact she had on my worldview. Our connection became a testament to the power of genuine, platonic relationships in enriching one's life. Florence had become a reminder that even in the absence of romantic love, a vibrant and meaningful connection could flourish.

Navigating my connection with Florence felt like performing a delicate balancing act, akin to walking a tightrope high above a vast chasm. This tightrope was my carefully constructed boundary, designed to keep our friendship intact without veering into the turbulent waters of romantic love. The balancing act required not only focus and precision but also an intuitive sense of equilibrium.

Maintaining this connection without crossing into the realm of romantic entanglement was crucial. I had already seen the pitfalls of letting emotions run unchecked, and I was determined to avoid them this time. Florence and I shared many moments of laughter and profound conversations, exploring the richness of life together. However, I was constantly vigilant, ensuring that our interactions remained within the confines of friendship.

The tightrope of our relationship was stretched between genuine camaraderie and the temptation of deeper affection. Each step I took along this wire was measured and deliberate. I allowed myself to enjoy Florence's company and the joy she brought into my life while keeping the lines clear and unblurred. The boundaries I set were not just barriers but also guiding principles that helped me maintain control.

Florence, for her part, respected this dynamic. Her carefree nature and spirited presence complemented my desire to keep things uncomplicated. She was fully aware of the nature of our connection and valued it for what it was—a meaningful friendship without the added weight of romantic expectations.

The ease with which I performed this balancing act was not due to a lack of feeling but rather a conscious choice to keep the relationship in its intended place. By focusing on the joy of our friendship and the unique experiences we shared, I was able to keep our connection both fulfilling and stable. The tightrope remained steady, and I continued walking it with a sense of accomplishment and peace.

In essence, managing this connection without allowing love to overshadow it was a triumph of control and intention. It demonstrated my ability to navigate complex emotions while preserving the integrity of a meaningful relationship. This careful balancing act became a testament to the power of deliberate action and the wisdom of knowing when to hold steady and when to let go.

Friendship over Love

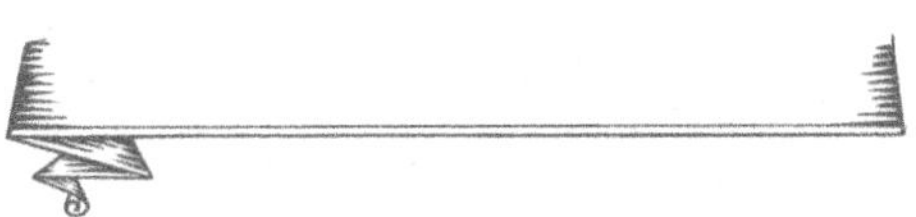

Florence was a force of nature—vibrant, magnetic, and endlessly captivating. From the moment we met, there was an undeniable connection between us, a synergy that felt almost effortless. Our friendship quickly blossomed into something rare and precious, built on trust, mutual respect, and a shared sense of humor that made every interaction feel light and refreshing. We had an unspoken understanding, a rhythm that allowed us to be completely ourselves in each other's presence.

The connection I shared with Florence was unlike anything I had experienced before. It wasn't just a simple friendship; it was a dynamic, invigorating bond that breathed life into my days. Florence was the kind of person who could light up a room just by being in it, and her presence in my life brought a level of joy and understanding that I hadn't known I was missing. Our relationship was easy, effortless, and full of mutual respect. We understood each other on a level that went beyond words, and that connection felt almost sacred.

As time went on, I began to notice subtle changes, not just in myself but in Florence as well. There were moments when her laughter lingered a little longer, when her eyes held mine with a softness that hinted at something more. It was nothing overt, just a spark—small, but unmistakable. I could sense that she, too, was feeling a pull, something that could easily grow into more if we let it.

Not so sure about her side but I definitely began to notice a shift within myself—subtle at first, but growing stronger with each passing day. Feelings started to stir, emotions that went beyond the boundaries of friendship. I found myself drawn to Florence in ways that were more than just platonic, and it scared me. I had seen what could happen when emotions like these took control; I had lived through it. And the last thing I wanted was to ruin something as beautiful as what we had.

But the more I tried to suppress these feelings, the more they seemed to grow. It wasn't long before I realized that I was at a crossroads. I could allow these emotions to evolve into something more, risking the purity of our friendship, or I could take a step back, preserving what we had by distancing myself from the temptation to take things further.

I knew that if I allowed those feelings to grow unchecked, it could destroy the very thing that made our bond so special. So, with great difficulty, I made the decision to bury those burgeoning emotions. I chose to pull back, not because I was afraid of what might happen, but because I valued our connection too much to let it be tainted by love.

Walking away from those feelings meant sacrificing something that could have been beautiful in its own right, but it also meant preserving the purity of what we already had. By choosing to keep our relationship within the bounds of friendship, I was ensuring that it remained strong, untarnished by the complications that love inevitably brings. It wasn't a decision made out of fear, but out of a deep understanding of what truly mattered. Florence and I continued our friendship, our bond growing even stronger, now fortified by the knowledge that we had something worth protecting—something far too valuable to risk losing to the unpredictable nature of romantic love.

As I began to maintain this distance from Florence, I couldn't help but notice that she sensed the subtle shift in our dynamic. It was as if she understood the unspoken tension, the delicate balance I was trying to maintain between preserving our friendship and preventing the growth of deeper feelings. Florence, in her usual graceful manner, allowed things to flow naturally, respecting the boundaries I was quietly setting.

This experience made me acutely aware of the complexity of human emotions. The connection I felt with Florence was genuine and profound, but it wasn't the type of connection I needed to foster. I realized that in order to maintain the purity of our friendship, I needed to find someone else with whom I could share those deeper emotional bonds. The importance of separating these different kinds of love became clearer than ever.

Florence's understanding of the situation and the way she effortlessly let things flow my way only deepened my respect for her. She didn't push or question the distance I was creating. Instead, she supported it, knowing that it was what I needed at the time. It was in this space of mutual respect and understanding that I found clarity—clarity about what I truly needed and the kind of emotional connection that would complement the friendship we had so carefully built.

This experience not only helped preserve what was beautiful between us but also reinforced my belief that some connections are meant to be cherished in their own unique way, without the complications of something as dangerous as love.

The Driving Force

As the conversation about Florence came to a close, a reflective silence settled over the terrace. The air was thick with unspoken thoughts, each of us lost in our own memories and musings. The city below was a mosaic of twinkling lights, a contrast to the deep emotions swirling between us.

I looked at Edward, his expression thoughtful, the weight of the stories I had shared evident in his eyes. He had always been the most perceptive, the one who felt things deeply but rarely showed it. Tonight, however, his sadness was palpable. He broke the silence, his voice soft yet tinged with an emotion he seldom displayed.

"Dad," he began, "I never knew how much you went through, how much you kept to yourself. I always saw you as strong, unshakeable... but I never realized what that strength cost you." His gaze met mine, and for a moment, we shared a connection that transcended words—a bond forged through shared pain and understanding.

Elsa, sensing the gravity of the moment, lightened the mood with her signature playfulness. "Well, Dad, you sure know how to keep secrets! But I think I like this version of you—a bit mysterious, a bit romantic, and definitely more human." She winked at me, a mischievous glint in her eye, and I couldn't help but smile. Her curiosity, however, was still piqued. "So, what happened next? You can't leave us hanging like this!"

I took a deep breath, feeling the weight of the story I had yet to tell. "Florence... she was a chapter that taught me a lot about myself, about love, and about the importance of controlling such a powerful force. But as much as that connection meant to me, it was Sarah who came into my life when I needed someone to help me rebuild. She was the one who allowed me to be myself, who gave me the freedom to embrace life once again."

As I mentioned Sarah's name, Sophia's eyes lit up with excitement. "Mom? You're talking about Mom now?" she interrupted, her voice filled with eagerness. The mere mention of her mother seemed to brighten her entire demeanor, her curiosity now focused on how our lives came together.

I smiled at her, knowing that the part of the story she was so curious about was one of both healing and growth. "Yes, Sophia," I began, my tone softening as I recalled the moment Sarah entered my life. "After everything I went through, after Florence and the realization that I needed to control the powerful force of love, Sarah came into my life like a gentle breeze—steady, calming, and exactly what I needed."

The story continued...

Chapter 4: Sarah

Exactly what the doctors order

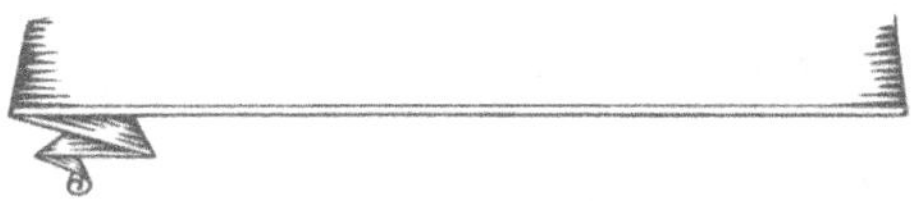

Just as I was beginning to appreciate the balance I had found with Florence, life took another unexpected turn. My family, unaware of the emotional upheaval I had gone through after Alice, began suggesting that it was time for me to consider remarriage. They believed that finding a partner would help me move forward, bring stability to my life, and reconnect me with the traditions that had always guided our family.

It was through these family connections that Sarah was introduced to me. She was everything my family hoped for—kind, supportive, and grounded. Unlike the whirlwind of emotions that had characterized my past, Sarah represented a calm, steady presence.

At first, I was hesitant. The emotional scars from Alice and Isabelle still lingered, and the connection I had with Florence, though carefully maintained as a friendship, made me wary of opening my heart again. Yet, Sarah's approach was different. She wasn't here to fill a void or heal a wound; she was simply there, offering a new chapter without the burden of the past.

I decided to give it a chance, not because I was searching for love, but because I was ready to embrace a different kind of connection—one that was more controlled, measured, and rooted in a mutual understanding of what we both wanted from life.

My family, blissfully unaware of the tumultuous journey I had endured since Alice, saw Sarah as the perfect match for me. Their encouragement was a gentle nudge toward a new beginning, a chance to embrace stability and rekindle the idea of marriage, this time with a more measured approach.

Sarah entered my life not as a whirlwind of passion but as a calm and steady presence. Our relationship blossomed with a sense of serenity and practicality. We approached our marriage with an understanding that only experience could provide. I was determined to apply the lessons learned from my past—the emotional turbulence with Isabelle, the connection with Florence, and the insights gained along the way.

This time, I knew how to shape our life together with intention. I had learned to control my love, to balance it with wisdom, and to ensure that our journey was smooth and harmonious. The chaotic elements of my past were replaced with a thoughtful approach to building a future with Sarah.

From the outset, Sarah's kindness was evident in the way she interacted with me. Her demeanor was soft, yet there was a quiet strength in her understanding. She approached our relationship with a rare blend of patience and insight. It was not just about the soothing words she offered or the gentle support she provided; it was her innate ability to see beyond my defenses and offer a genuine partnership that struck a chord with me.

In Sarah, I found someone who perfectly fit into the role of the partner I had longed for—a partner who could meet me halfway without overwhelming me. Her soft-spoken nature and empathetic responses made conversations flow effortlessly, creating a safe space where I could finally let down my guard. Sarah didn't just listen; she actively engaged with my thoughts and emotions, fostering a sense of mutual respect that was both reassuring and invigorating.

The transition from my past experiences to life with Sarah was marked by a profound shift. With Florence, there had been a palpable tension due to the emotional depth of our connection, which had made navigating our bond complicated. However, with Sarah, the initial stages of our relationship were characterized by a sense of simplicity and ease.

My feelings for her were still forming, which allowed me to manage them with a clarity and control that had previously eluded me.

This new chapter with Sarah was less about the tumultuous highs and lows and more about finding a steady rhythm. Her presence helped me navigate the complexities of love with a newfound sense of balance. I was able to approach our relationship with a clearer vision, shaped by the lessons learned from past experiences. With Sarah, I discovered that love could be both profound and manageable, that it could be a source of comfort rather than a chaotic force.

The Insight

The early days with Sarah were marked by a subtle but profound shift in my life. Meeting her wasn't like falling into a tempestuous storm; it was more like stepping into a calm, serene space that was refreshingly new and reassuring. Our initial interactions were simple yet revealing, and as I look back, I realize how crucial those moments were in shaping our future together.

Sarah and I met through family connections, a serendipitous introduction orchestrated by well-meaning relatives who knew that I needed someone who could bring stability and balance into my life. From our very first conversation, I felt an inexplicable ease around her. It was as though her presence was a balm to the turbulence I had experienced.

Our early dates were filled with light conversations and shared laughter. We would visit quaint cafes, where we talked about everything and nothing, discovering each other's likes and dislikes. Sarah had a way of listening intently, making me feel heard and understood in a way that was both comforting and invigorating. Her demeanor was calm and her approach to life was gentle, which contrasted sharply with the whirlwind of emotions I had navigated before.

One of my fondest memories from those early days was the way Sarah would manage our outings with such grace. Whether we were strolling through a park or enjoying a quiet dinner, she had this knack for creating a relaxed atmosphere, where I could just be myself without the weight of past experiences hanging over me. It was during these moments that I began to realize the depth of her character. She was someone who didn't seek to control or demand, but rather to understand and support.

Building our relationship felt like constructing a delicate masterpiece. Sarah's ability to give me space while also showing her affection was something I hadn't experienced before. She allowed me to take things at my own pace, without rushing or forcing anything. This was particularly important for me, given my history of intense and sometimes overwhelming relationships. With Sarah, the pressure was off, and I could enjoy the simplicity of building a life together, one day at a time.

We gradually began to weave our lives together, blending our routines and dreams. Sarah's presence became a steadying influence, and the small things we did together—like decorating our home or planning family outings—felt more significant than I could have imagined. Each shared experience, from setting up a cozy living room to cooking meals together, contributed to a sense of partnership and mutual respect.

What stood out the most during this period was Sarah's unwavering support. She embraced her role with an intuitive understanding of what I needed. Whether it was managing household responsibilities or navigating the complexities of parenting, she approached everything with a calm demeanor that helped me find my own equilibrium.

As our relationship evolved, so did my appreciation for the unique balance Sarah brought into my life. She was not just a partner but a companion who helped me build a stable foundation for our future. Her gentle influence allowed me to embrace life's uncertainties with confidence, knowing that I had someone steadfast by my side.

Sarah and I, having found a profound connection in each other, were committed to moving forward and building a life that was both fulfilling and secure. After the tumultuous experiences of our past, we both yearned for stability and a sense of purpose. Together, we laid out plans for the future, infused with the hope of a fresh start. We were not just seeking to rebuild but to create something truly special—something that would stand the test of time.

The arrival of Elsa and Sophia marked the beginning of this new chapter. Their presence was a blessing that brought an unparalleled depth to our relationship. Holding them for the first time, I felt a surge of emotions—a mix of pride, love, and an overwhelming sense of responsibility. These little girls became the heart of our home, their laughter and innocence filling our lives with joy and meaning.

As we navigated the early days of parenthood, Sarah's support was unwavering. She was not just a partner but a pillar of strength, balancing the demands of motherhood with grace and dedication. Her ability to manage our home, care for the children, and still make time for us was nothing short of remarkable. It was during these moments that our bond deepened, as we both realized how much we complemented each other.

Raising Elsa and Sophia together was an experience that strengthened our relationship in ways we hadn't anticipated. Every little milestone—from their first steps to their first words—was celebrated with a sense of unity that brought us closer. The small moments of joy, like watching them play together or tucking them into bed at night, were reminders of the life we were building—one filled with love, laughter, and a shared purpose.

We made it a point to cherish the everyday moments. Whether it was planning family outings, decorating the house together, or simply enjoying a quiet evening at home, we found contentment in the life we were creating. Sarah's nurturing nature and her ability to make our house a home brought a sense of peace and happiness that had been missing for so long. Our bond was no longer just about the two of us—it was about the family we had created, and the future we were shaping for Elsa and Sophia.

With each passing day, our connection grew stronger, and the love we shared became the foundation on which we built our lives. Sarah's presence brought stability and comfort, and as we navigated the challenges of life together, our relationship evolved into something truly beautiful. Our plans for the future, once filled with uncertainty, were now grounded in the shared belief that we could face anything as long as we had each other. Elsa and Sophia were not just our daughters; they were the embodiment of the love and dedication we had poured into our relationship, and with them, our bond was unbreakable.

These early days with Sarah were a testament to the power of patience and understanding in a relationship. They set the stage for a love that was not only steady and enduring but also deeply fulfilling. It was clear that, with Sarah, I had found a connection that could weather any storm, a love that was both grounded and nurturing.

Sarah and Edward

From the moment Sarah entered our lives, her warmth and kindness extended beyond her relationship with me and reached deeply into Edward's life. The transition into the role of a stepmother was not just a formal change in our family structure, but a journey that Sarah approached with genuine compassion and a heartfelt commitment.

Sarah's interactions with Edward were marked by an immediate and authentic connection. Despite the initial complexities of blending our families, Sarah's approach was characterized by an unwavering patience and a sincere desire to build a bond with Edward. She understood that her role was not to replace his mother but to become an important and supportive figure in his life.

In the early days, Sarah made a conscious effort to engage with Edward on his terms. She took the time to understand his interests, listen to his stories, and be present in his world. Whether it was participating in his hobbies, attending his school events, or simply spending quiet time together, Sarah's involvement was consistent and heartfelt. She did not rush the process or impose her on Edward but allowed their relationship to develop naturally over time.

One of the most significant aspects of Sarah's approach was her ability to offer emotional support without overstepping boundaries. She recognized the delicate balance of being a stepmother and chose to offer guidance and affection in ways that respected Edward's existing relationship and his own pace of adaptation. Her empathy and understanding provided Edward with a sense of security and acceptance, which was crucial during this transitional period.

Sarah's efforts to create a positive environment for Edward were also reflected in the home they shared. She thoughtfully included Edward in family activities and decision-making processes, ensuring that he felt valued and involved. Her attention to detail, from planning family outings to setting up a space in the home that reflected Edward's personality, demonstrated her commitment to making him feel at home.

The connection Sarah built with Edward was a significant relief for me. It eased the burden I had carried for not being with my son's mother. Knowing that Edward had a loving and supportive figure in his life provided me with a sense of comfort and reassurance. Sarah's ability to form such a meaningful relationship with Edward alleviated some of the guilt and concerns I had about his well-being, allowing me to focus on navigating our new life together with greater peace of mind.

Over time, the bond between Sarah and Edward deepened, marked by moments of shared joy and mutual respect. Their relationship evolved from initial uncertainty to a genuine affection. Edward began to appreciate Sarah not just as a stepmother but as a trusted friend and confidante. Their interactions were characterized by a playful ease and a growing mutual understanding, reflecting the positive impact of Sarah's nurturing presence.

Sarah's role in Edward's life was more than just a supportive figure; it became a source of strength for him. Her consistent encouragement and genuine care provided Edward with a stable foundation during a period of significant change. Through her actions and interactions, Sarah demonstrated that family is not solely defined by biological connections but also by the love and support shared among its members.

The transformation in Edward's relationship with Sarah was a testament to her dedication and the love she brought into our lives. It was a journey of integrating into an established family dynamic with grace and sensitivity, and it was marked by the deep affection that naturally grew between them. Sarah's role as a stepmother was not just about fulfilling a position but about enriching our family with her compassion, understanding, and unwavering commitment.

As we moved forward together, Sarah's bond with Edward became a cornerstone of our blended family's strength. It was a relationship built on trust, respect, and genuine love—a relationship that reflected the positive impact of Sarah's role in our lives and the deep connections we forged as a family.

Rediscovering Vulnerabilities

During my time with Sarah, I experienced a profound transformation, both personally and emotionally. The evolution was not merely a result of our relationship but also a reflection of the changes I underwent as a person.

Before meeting Sarah, I had built walls around myself, shaped by past experiences and emotional struggles. My relationship with Alice had been intense and transformative, yet it left me feeling exposed and wary of fully embracing new emotions. With Isabelle, I had learned to guard my heart more diligently, navigating love with a sense of detachment. Meeting Sarah was a turning point. Her genuine kindness and unwavering support began to break down the barriers I had carefully constructed. Sarah's ability to understand and accept me for who I was, without judgment or pretense, gradually allowed me to rediscover vulnerability. I started to open up more, sharing my thoughts and feelings without fear of being misunderstood or rejected. This newfound openness was a significant step in my personal evolution.

Sarah's presence in my life brought a sense of balance that had been missing for a long time. Her gentle nature and thoughtful approach to our relationship created an environment where I felt both grounded and uplifted. I learned to appreciate the subtle yet profound ways in which she balanced her role as a partner and a stepmother. Sarah's calm demeanor and her ability to navigate challenges with grace taught me the value of maintaining equilibrium in both personal and familial dynamics. Her approach helped me understand the importance of balance in relationships, emphasizing that love thrives when it is nurtured with patience, respect, and mutual understanding.

Sarah's patience and understanding were pivotal in shaping my growth. Her ability to handle situations with a calm and measured approach encouraged me to adopt similar qualities. I found myself becoming more patient, not just with Sarah but with others around me. This shift was particularly noticeable in my interactions with Edward and in managing the complexities of blended family dynamics. Sarah's influence helped me develop a greater sense of empathy and tolerance, both of which were crucial in navigating the challenges of our evolving family life.

One of the most profound changes during my time with Sarah was the rekindling of joy in everyday moments. Sarah had a way of finding beauty in simplicity and celebrating the small, everyday pleasures of life. Her approach reminded me of the importance of savoring these moments and finding joy in the present. I began to appreciate the value of creating and cherishing simple, joyful experiences—whether it was through shared activities, spontaneous adventures, or quiet moments together. This reconnection with the joy of living contributed significantly to my personal growth and overall well-being.

Sarah's role in our relationship extended beyond her support; it encompassed a collaborative spirit that enriched our lives. We faced challenges and celebrated successes together, learning to work as a team to build a harmonious life. Her collaborative approach inspired me to adopt a more cooperative and inclusive mindset in our relationship. This spirit of collaboration extended to our family life, where we worked together to create a nurturing environment for Edward and to integrate our lives seamlessly.

The evolution I experienced with Sarah also involved embracing change with grace. Our relationship required adaptability as we blended our families and navigated the intricacies of our new life together. Sarah's ability to approach change with optimism and resilience served as a model for how to handle transitions gracefully. This adaptability helped me become more comfortable with change, allowing me to face challenges with a more positive and proactive attitude.

Ultimately, my time with Sarah instilled in me a renewed sense of purpose. Her presence and the love we shared gave me a clearer perspective on what truly mattered in life. I became more focused on nurturing meaningful relationships, pursuing personal growth, and contributing positively to our family. This renewed sense of purpose was a driving force in my continued evolution and in the way I approached life moving forward.

Behind every successful man, there is a woman

Sarah's unwavering support and nurturing presence created a stable foundation that allowed me to redirect my energy and focus more effectively on my professional growth. Her ability to manage household responsibilities and her commitment to creating a harmonious home environment significantly alleviated the stress and distractions that had previously affected my work.

Sarah's thoughtful approach to managing our home life meant that I could dedicate more time and energy to my professional pursuits. Her organization and efficiency in handling daily responsibilities—ranging from coordinating family activities to managing household tasks—provided me with the mental and emotional space needed to concentrate on my career. With fewer distractions and a well-organized home environment, I found it easier to immerse myself in my work, leading to increased productivity and a clearer focus on my professional goals.

Sarah's belief in my abilities and her encouragement played a crucial role in boosting my confidence and motivation. Her positive reinforcement and understanding of the demands of my profession helped me feel more secure in pursuing ambitious projects and career advancements. Sarah's support was not just about managing day-to-day life but also about actively encouraging me to push beyond my comfort zone and seize new opportunities. Her faith in my potential fueled my drive to achieve more professionally, leading to a renewed sense of purpose and determination in my career.

One of the significant benefits of Sarah's support was her ability to maintain a balance between work and personal life. Her presence allowed me to establish clearer boundaries between my professional and personal spheres, reducing the risk of burnout and ensuring that I could fully engage in both areas. Sarah's understanding of the importance of work-life balance meant that I could focus on my career without sacrificing the quality of our family life. This balance was instrumental in helping me excel professionally while still being present and attentive at home.

Sarah's role extended beyond practical support; she provided emotional stability that was vital for my professional success. Her calming presence and empathetic approach helped me navigate the pressures and challenges of my career with a more resilient mindset. Knowing that I had a reliable and understanding partner at home gave me the confidence to tackle professional obstacles and pursue my goals with a greater sense of assurance. This emotional stability was a cornerstone of my professional growth, enabling me to approach my work with a clearer, more focused mindset.

Sarah's support also included facilitating opportunities for my professional development. Whether it was by encouraging me to attend workshops, pursue additional training, or explore new career paths, her proactive involvement was instrumental in my growth. Her willingness to support my ambitions and her practical assistance in managing the logistics of professional commitments allowed me to take advantage of developmental opportunities that contributed to my career advancement.

Sarah's influence encouraged me to adopt a growth mindset, both personally and professionally. Her positive outlook and constructive feedback helped me view challenges as opportunities for growth rather than obstacles. This mindset shift was crucial for my professional development, as it empowered me to approach projects with creativity, resilience, and a willingness to learn from experiences. Sarah's role in fostering this mindset was a key factor in my ability to achieve new milestones and progress in my career.

"Behind every successful man, there is a woman" and for me, that woman was Sarah.

The Conclusion

The cold steel of the gun lay on the terrace beside me, a silent witness to the tumultuous journey that had brought me to this point. Its presence was deliberate, a symbol of the power that love held over my life—a power that could either heal or destroy. As the wind whispered through the city below, I could feel the weight of the decisions I had made, each one etched into the metal of that gun, a reminder of how dangerously close love could come to consuming everything.

It wasn't just an object; it was a metaphor for the battles I had fought within myself. The gun represented the moments where love had been so overwhelming, so intense, that it felt like a double-edged sword—capable of cutting through all pretenses but also leaving deep scars. In my hand, it was heavy, not just in its physical weight but in the burden it symbolized—the burden of choices, the burden of control.

Edward's eyes often drifted to the gun, his youthful face reflecting a mix of curiosity and concern. He knew it wasn't just an idle prop; it was a part of the story, part of my narrative that he was only beginning to understand. The gun had been there through the darkest nights, when love had pushed me to the edge, challenging my very will to carry on. It had seen the despair, the anger, and the moments of clarity that had eventually led me to this terrace, surrounded by my children, on the precipice of telling my story.

As Elsa's voice cut through the tension, lightening the mood with her playful curiosity, I found myself easing the grip on the gun, placing it back on the concrete. It was a reminder that, while love was powerful and needed to be controlled, it didn't have to lead to destruction. The gun had once symbolized an escape, a way out when love became too much to bear. But now, it was just a relic of a past I had conquered, a past that had taught me that true strength lay not in succumbing to the darkness but in finding the balance to navigate it.

As I reflect on the tapestry of my life, woven with threads of intense love, painful detachment, and transformative connections, I realize that each chapter has been instrumental in shaping my understanding of what love truly means. Each experience, laying the foundation for a better understanding of controlling the outcomes love can cause.

My time with Alice taught me the intoxicating magic of love unrestrained, where dreams and reality intertwined in a whirlwind of emotions. The passion and spontaneity we shared were a testament to love's capacity to enchant and captivate. As beautiful as this love was, it was wild, one that is hard to control and maintain. This kind of love can break you to the point where death seems a priority over the pain it inflicts.

My love with Alice was wild and untamed, a force that defied reason and thrived on the intensity of the moment. From the very beginning, it was clear that our connection was something fierce and passionate, something that burned brightly but dangerously close to the edge.

Our relationship was a whirlwind, filled with the kind of highs that make you feel invincible and the kind of lows that leave you gasping for air. We were two souls drawn together by an inexplicable force, and when we were together, nothing else seemed to matter. But that same force that brought us together also threatened to tear us apart.

The intensity of our love was exhilarating, but it was also exhausting. We fed off each other's energy, pushing boundaries and testing limits, often without considering the consequences. It was a love that consumed everything in its path, leaving little room for anything else. In our quest to experience it all, we sometimes lost sight of the balance needed to sustain a healthy relationship.

As thrilling as it was, our love with Alice was also perilous. The very qualities that made it so electrifying—its spontaneity, its passion—were the same ones that made it so volatile. The wildness of our connection meant that emotions were often heightened, and misunderstandings could quickly escalate into something much more dangerous.

Looking back, I realize that while our love was a powerful force, it was also a reminder of the need for control. The wild nature of our relationship with Alice taught me that love, if left unchecked, could easily spiral into something destructive. It was a lesson that, though learned the hard way, became a cornerstone in understanding how to navigate the complexities of love in the future.

With Isabelle, I encountered a love that was more measured and cautious, marked by a growing realization of sacrifice and the heavy burden of potential regret. It was a period of emotional wrestling, where I grappled with my own vulnerabilities and the harsh truths of a relationship that seemed to demand too much. It was the kind that required sacrifices. It was smooth, yet complicated, challenging one's ability to interpret the outcomes of the future. As beautiful as it seemed, it had the power to question one's own decision, to compare choices and lead to regrets ultimately.

The love I shared with Isabelle was unlike any other—unpredictable, raw, and intense. It was a love that kept me on edge, never knowing what the next moment would bring. With Isabelle, emotions ran deep, and the line between passion and fear was often blurred. This unpredictability made our connection thrilling yet exhausting, as I found myself caught between the highs of our bond and the looming anxiety of what might come next.

The intensity of our relationship forced me to confront my own vulnerabilities, revealing how easily love could spiral out of control when not properly managed. While our time together was marked by unforgettable moments, it also taught me the crucial lesson that love, when unchecked, could lead to emotional turmoil. This experience with

Isabelle ultimately became a turning point, highlighting the importance of balance and the need for control to prevent love from becoming overwhelming and consuming.

Florence came into my life as a vibrant contrast, a beacon of joy and spontaneity that rekindled my appreciation for life's simple pleasures. Her presence reminded me of the lighter side of love—one that doesn't necessarily need to be laden with deep emotional entanglements but can be fulfilling in its own right. It was calm, composed and balanced.

The lesson I learned from my time with Florence was profound. Our connection was a rare sanctuary, built on mutual comfort and understanding. It was effortless and natural, something I deeply cherished. But with that comfort came a fear—the fear that trying to deepen our bond might disrupt its quiet beauty. The thought of changing what was already so perfect seemed risky.

Florence taught me that some relationships thrive in their simplicity. They don't need to be redefined or intensified; sometimes, the best love is one that remains untouched, appreciated for the peace it brings. This experience shaped my understanding of love—not as something to be poked or intensified, but as something to be carefully nurtured, knowing when to let it be and when to let it grow.

And then it was Sarah, who became the anchor I needed. Her gentle strength and understanding allowed me to embrace life and love on my own terms. She provided the balance and stability I sought, demonstrating that love, when guided by empathy and respect, can create a harmonious space for personal growth and mutual support.

Sarah's love didn't demand or consume; it complemented and empowered. This allowed me to finally understand that love is most powerful when it is balanced. It requires neither the reckless abandon I experienced with Alice nor the guarded detachment I felt after Isabelle. Instead, it thrived on mutual respect and a deep understanding of each other's needs and boundaries.

Through Sarah, I learned that love, when controlled and nurtured, becomes a force that not only enriches life but also provides the clarity and stability needed to face its challenges. It was with her that I truly grasped the art of controlling love—not by suppressing it, but by channeling it in ways that brought out the best in both of us.

Each experience, with its unique challenges and lessons, has contributed to a richer, more nuanced understanding of love. I've learned that love is not a singular concept but a multifaceted journey that evolves with us. It is shaped by our interactions, our trials, and our triumphs.

As the city lights begin to flicker below us, the night air carries a crispness that seems to sharpen our reflections. I sit on the terrace with Edward, Elsa, and Sophia, the conversation having drifted naturally to the topic of love—a theme that has been central to my life's journey.

Edward, eyes curious and earnest, asks, "Dad, after everything you've been through, what do you think love really is? How do you understand it now?"

I pause, gathering my thoughts. "Love," I begin, "is an incredibly powerful force, almost like an untamed beast. It has the capacity to bring immense joy and deep pain. It drives us, fuels our passions, and influences our decisions in profound ways."

I look out over the city, trying to find the right words. "Imagine love as a high-performance engine. It has tremendous potential, but without proper control, it can become dangerous. It needs the right amount of throttle to function effectively. If you push it too hard, it can become overwhelming and lead to chaos. If you don't engage it enough, it might stall and not reach its full potential."

I glance at Edward, who seems intrigued. "With Alice, love felt like a storm—wild and all-consuming. It swept through my life with such force that it was both thrilling and overwhelming. Just as a storm needs to be respected for its power, our love demanded a balance to keep from spiraling into chaos."

Turning to Elsa, who's listening closely, I continue, "When I was with Isabelle, love was more like an iceberg. It was massive and cold, with much of my emotions hidden beneath a surface of detachment. The iceberg showed me that while keeping control was necessary, ignoring the depths of my feelings only led to emotional isolation."

Sophia's curiosity shines through as she asks, "And what about Florence? How did she fit into all this?"

I smile, recalling the vibrant energy Florence brought into my life. "Florence was like a firework—bright and full of life. Her presence ignited a sense of wonder and joy that I hadn't felt in a long time. It was dazzling, but I knew that managing such brilliance was essential to ensure it didn't overshadow the stability I had worked so hard to build."

I take a deep breath and look at them with a sense of fulfillment. "And now with Sarah, love has become like tending to a garden. It's delicate and requires care, but it's also steady and nurturing. Her understanding has provided a stable ground where love can grow at its own pace, balanced and harmonious."

I pause for a moment, letting these thoughts settle in. "Each phase of my life has taught me that love is incredibly powerful. It can be a storm that demands respect, an iceberg that needs understanding, a firework that requires careful management, or a garden that needs nurturing. What's crucial is finding the right balance—controlling its power so that it enhances our lives rather than overwhelms us."

As I finish sharing my reflections, the terrace door creaks open, and Sarah steps out, adding a touch of elegance to the evening air. She's draped in a stunning black saree that flows gracefully around her, the fabric shimmering softly under the terrace lights. Her calm demeanor is matched by the serene beauty of her face, which glows with a natural radiance. The gentle drape of the saree accentuates her poise, and her eyes, framed by delicate makeup, sparkle with a hint of mischief.

"Are we done with this secret meeting, or can we finally head to the book signing?" Sarah teased, her eyes sparkling with affection as she looked at us. Elsa, ever the mischief-maker, couldn't resist. "Does Sarah know about Florence?" she whispered loudly enough for everyone to hear.

Sarah raised an eyebrow, clearly confused. "Florence? Who's that?" We all burst into laughter, the tension of the night dissolving in that shared moment of humor.

I chuckled softly, shaking my head. "Looks like we've managed to keep some stories exclusive to certain circles but let's save it for another time."

We all share a light laugh, the mood lifting as we prepare to leave. Sarah's calm, beautiful presence contrasts with the lively conversation, her serene smile adding warmth to the evening. She shakes her head with a smile, her laughter soft and inviting. "I guess I'll have to hear that story another time. For now, let's head to the book signing before it gets too late."

I glance back at the terrace, where the gun and coffee cup remain—a quiet reminder of the evening's reflective moments. With a final look around, I gather my thoughts and rise from my seat.

"Alright, let's go," I say, ushering everyone toward the door. "It's time for the book signing, and I'm ready to embrace whatever comes next."

We head inside, leaving the terrace behind, its quiet remnants a testament to the journey we've shared. The evening promises new beginnings, and with a shared laugh and the company of those I love, I feel ready to face the next chapter of our lives.